HUMBLE AND KIND

THE STORY OF
FRANK AND FAYE CALDWELL

MYRON L. CALDWELL

Carpenter's Son Publishing

Published by Carpenter's Son Publishing, Franklin, Tennessee

Published in association with Shane Crabtree of Christian Book Services, LLC
www.christianbookservices.com

Edited by Bob Irvin

Interior and Cover Design by Suzanne Lawing

Printed in the United States of America

978-1-954437-74-6

ACKNOWLEDGMENTS

This book would not be possible without my parents, Frank and Faye Caldwell, whose journey through life inspired me to record their story.

I owe a big thanks to many people who helped with this book, especially my wife, Dorothy, and daughters, Heather and Shannon. They graciously listened to my ideas, edited early drafts, and made several helpful suggestions. My brothers, Frank Jr., Tommy, and Dan, shared stories and memories about our parents and what it was like growing up "in the country" on North Hoskins Road. During a lengthy telephone call in October 2020, my uncle, Carl Lawing, patiently answered a number of my questions and discussed life in Kendall Mill Village. Nearing the completion of the book and sensing the need to get affirmation from others about the lives and character of Frank and Faye Caldwell, I turned to their grandchildren. Danita, Jennifer, Carrie, Andrew, Chad, Amanda, Tyler, Heather, Shannon, and Katie hit the mark, contributing stories of their grandparents, which comprise the chapter "In Their Own Words." Finally, a big thanks to the Carpenter's Son Publishing team of Shane Crabtree, Bob Irvin, and Suzanne Lawing for their support and expertise throughout the publishing process.

ABOUT THE COVER

The Caldwell farmhouse in Mecklenburg County, North Carolina on Belt Road between Hoskins and Beatties Ford Road, was the home of WB and Lenora Caldwell and their 11 children. Situated on a 100-acre farm, it was also the site of Caldwell's Sausage, a business owned and managed by WB and, later, his sons, Tom and Albert. The business, which originated around the turn of the twentieth century, operated from the basement of the farmhouse for almost 60 years. Albert, who inherited the home after his mother passed away, commissioned this sketch for a Christmas card.

For my grandchildren, Sawyer and Grace, and future generations of Frank and Faye Caldwell's descendants.

CONTENTS

PREFACE

In 2005 I compiled a brief story about my parents, Frank Wilson and Faye Lawing Caldwell, presenting it to them as a gift for their 65th wedding anniversary. Knowing Daddy was in failing health, I wanted to document their life while he was still living. He loved the story and referred to it as "the tribute that Myron wrote." In many ways that is what I intended: a tribute to my parents and their legacy of living a good life while enriching the lives of many others. However, I also was interested in preserving, for their grandchildren, their history and the times in which they lived.

Daddy died on February 17, 2006, less than a year after celebrating 65 years of marriage to Mama. His last days were filled with peace and grace as he was given one last gift: time to say goodbye to his family and friends before passing away. He courageously faced death, comforting others during his last days more than we comforted him. Mama found herself living alone for the first time in her life following his death. Moving away from her longtime home on North Hoskins Road to the Oakdale community a few miles away, our family was concerned about how she would adjust to this significant change. There was no need to worry as she lived happily in her new home, close to good friends and her church. She later moved to an assisted living community and passed away on February 4, 2011 after a brief illness.

After retiring in 2016, I began researching my family history dating back to the colonial days of Mecklenburg County. As my research progressed, I discovered stories about Mama and Daddy, the history of their families, and the events that influenced and shaped their lives. This book, years in the making, includes a little of that history, a bit of the family lore, and a dose of genealogy. Most importantly, however, it is the story of their journey through life.

My brothers and I were blessed to have loving parents. Mama and Daddy were ordinary people who never sought or received a great deal of attention or notoriety. Two simple individuals, they were thankful for what they had, and they never worried about what they did not need. Happy to have a loving family and a home they could call their own, Mama and Daddy were forever humble and kind.

One

INTRODUCING FRANK AND FAYE

Tom Brokaw, the former NBC network news anchor, wrote a book titled *The Greatest Generation*. He was referring to the generation born in the early decades of the twentieth century that came of age during the Great Depression, fought a world war, created great economic wealth, and seeded the American dream for future generations. Frank Wilson Caldwell and Bertie Faye Lawing were part of this generation, born in rural Mecklenburg County in North Carolina during the early 1920s, a time of rapid growth and renewed optimism in the U.S. following the end of World War I.

The 1920s, frequently called the Roaring Twenties, was a time in which many individuals, especially those in the larger cities, were living life to the fullest. Consumers, eager to spend more freely than ever, took out loans to buy automobiles, radios, telephones, and other modern conveniences. Investors eagerly poured money into the financial markets, bidding up stock prices on Wall Street. Entertainment was on the rise with the construction of hundreds of movie theatres and radio stations in cities and towns across the U.S. Major city skylines rapidly changed with new buildings reaching higher and higher in downtown

*Charlotte's Independence Square in the 1920s looking north on Tryon Street.
Includes the Independence Building, Kress 5, 10, and 25 Store, Southern
Public Utilities Streetcar, and Ivey's Department Store. Photo courtesy of the
Robinson-Spangler Carolina Room, Charlotte Mecklenburg Library.*

business districts. Charlotte, the largest city in Mecklenburg County, prospered as well, adding new buildings, hotels, churches, hospitals, and movie theatres. The city's downtown bustled with automobiles, electric street cars, and new department stores filled with shoppers. In short, life was good in the 1920s.

By the end of the decade, however, the good life would abruptly end and the bills would come due.

The years of easy money and speculative bets on Wall Street had run their course. All of this led to the stock market crash in October 1929. A financial panic ensued with lenders calling their outstanding loans and account holders making a run on banks. The U.S. was not prepared for the fallout, a Great Depression, which would spread throughout the world and continue to negatively impact the country's economic standing for years to come. Massive numbers of people were suddenly unemployed, losing their life savings, homes, and possessions. The good times and prosperity turned into misery and hardship as families struggled to put food on the table to feed their children.

Perhaps it was providential that most of Frank and Faye's generation were not old enough to fully appreciate the good times of the Roaring Twenties. Instead, they came of age in the midst of the extended economic depression, living with their families through lean times and financial struggles into the early 1940s. Perhaps those difficult times were necessary to prepare this generation for an even greater struggle to come—a second world war. There is no doubt the lessons learned in those years made this generation self-sufficient and thrifty while instilling a strong sense of accountability, bringing people together to help in times of despair.

Living through those challenging times left an indelible mark on Frank and Faye, shaping their beliefs and values for the rest of their lives. Strong financial stewards, they learned to pay cash for purchases, save for a rainy day, and, most importantly, make do with what they had or simply do without. Those experiences molded them into hardworking, patriotic, God-fearing individuals. It also gave them a lasting appreciation for what they considered the most important things in life: faith, family, and friends.

Frank and Faye met in 1939 under a streetlight as Frank was driving through Kendall Village, a textile mill community in Mecklenburg County. As Frank recalled at a family Christmas gathering in 2004, he had seen a girl from Paw Creek playing basketball and asked her out on a date. Concluding after one date that he was no longer interested in that young lady, he noticed Faye and set in motion a plan to meet her. Yes, just like today, boys in 1939 were out riding around in cars looking for girls.

A farmer's son, Frank was a country boy who lived between the Hoskins Community and Beatties Ford Road in north Mecklenburg County. His family of eight resided on a small farm in a two-story wooden farmhouse on a dusty dirt road. Frank's parents, Thomas (Tom) Parks Caldwell and Azalee Wilson Caldwell, tended chickens and cows, grew vegetables, and sold milk, butter, and eggs as part of their livelihood. Faye grew up in the Thrift Community, part of Paw Creek Township in western Mecklenburg County, in a mill village. Charlie Mack Lawing, her father, worked in the cotton mill, while her mother, Carrie Blankenship Lawing, had her hands full caring for ten children.

Faye was a pretty, brown-eyed girl of fifteen when she met Frank. Tall, with long dark hair, she had a bright smile that could light up a room. Frank, a thin, rangy teenage boy, stood six feet two inches and weighed about 150 pounds. He was a sharp dresser, typically wearing a coat, tie, and hat while sporting well shined shoes. Faye often recalled how she was impressed by Frank's neat and clean appearance, an attribute she highly valued. Typical dates included trips to the movie theater or the soda shop for an ice cream.

Frank and Faye Caldwell, early 1940s.

The farm boy and the mill village girl fell in love and eloped to York, South Carolina on September 5, 1940. Frank was a month shy of 20 while Faye was only 16 years old. Though these were their true ages, the marriage license states Frank was 25 and Faye 18. No one knew of the age discrepancies on the marriage license until after Frank passed away in 2006. When asked about the conflicting ages, Faye simply smiled in her usual way, offering no explanation. Obviously, none was really needed.

The year 1940, when Frank and Faye married, was one of turmoil and uncertainty. The U.S. was still struggling economically and growing more concerned about the war raging across Europe and Asia. Mecklenburg County, while still predominantly rural, was growing rapidly, having doubled its population since 1920. Charlotte, the largest city in the county with 100,000 citizens, sat at the epicenter of the Carolina textile industry with 770 mills operating within a 100-mile radius. The city was well positioned as the manufacturing and distribution center of the Carolinas; a new municipal airport and four railroads served the region. The Charlotte Chamber proudly touted the city's 320 miles of streets, highlighting that 146 were paved. The city's slogan, "Watch Charlotte Grow," was a rather appropriate one considering the growth to come in future decades.

Frank and Faye, two ordinary people, lived during an extraordinary time. Their story, shared together for more than 65 years, is a simple one. It is based on faith, hard work, perseverance, and love.

Two

THE MECKLENBURG CONNECTION

Mecklenburg County lies in the western part of the Piedmont area of North Carolina, situated between the Appalachian Mountains in the west and the coastal plains to the east. Charlotte, with its professional sports teams, uptown skyscrapers, and several corporations with S&P 500 headquarters, is the county seat and one of the fastest-growing cities in the U.S.; it had a population approaching one million as of 2022. Considering the continuous development and influx of thousands of new residents each year, it is difficult to imagine how this area appeared around 1740 when first inhabited by European settlers. The crude log houses with dirt floors, rolling landscapes, abundant wildlife, and a small population of hardworking pioneer families are too often forgotten. The promise of a better life was top of mind for those early settlers who came from Europe and other American colonies to this wild and unspoiled land.

Among those who came were Daniel Caldwell and William Lawing, the first of Frank and Faye's ancestors to live in Mecklenburg County.

The first European settlers arriving in North Carolina came primarily from England, establishing settlements along the coast in the early 1700s. Farther inland, to the west, the interior of the colony remained largely unsettled by Europeans for several decades; tribes of native Cherokee and Catawba Indians lived there along the rivers and creeks. The native peoples inhabited small communities, hunting wild game, growing corn along the waterways, and cutting trails from the mountains to the coast. For many years the only white men to travel into the North Carolina interior were traders who bartered with the natives, exchanging finished goods for animal hides. Unfortunately for the natives, settlers soon followed the traders into the colony, quickly displacing the Cherokee and Catawba population.

Around 1740 the first white settlers began to arrive in what is now Mecklenburg County. At the time, Mecklenburg was part of Anson County, a vast land mass extending west of the North Carolina coastal plains. These early settlers were true pioneers who traveled in covered wagons, trekking along the Great Philadelphia Wagon Road that ran south from Pennsylvania through Virginia and into the Carolinas. It was a long, difficult journey through untamed wilderness on a road that was nothing more than a number of rough, connected trails previously used by the natives and a few white traders.

Over the next several decades thousands more arrived. Some traveled from the north along the same wagon road while others came in ships from Europe, disembarking in the port cities of Wilmington and Charleston and continuing over land. These new pioneers were largely German Lutherans and Scotch-Irish Presbyterians seeking religious freedom, better economic opportunities, and land in the sparsely populated colony. By 1760 several small villages with houses and farms were established, and these were typically centered around local churches in the community. As the population grew, a new county, Mecklenburg, was partitioned from Anson County in 1762. Within the same decade, the town of Charlotte was incorporated and designated as the county seat. At that time the town consisted of nothing more than a small log courthouse and a few houses at the intersection of two dusty roads.

Sketch of Charlottetown as it appeared in 1767 by Kenneth Whitsett, a Charlotte artist and Frank's second cousin. The cross paths East-West and North-South are present day Trade and Tryon Streets respectively, intersecting at Charlotte's square. Sketch courtesy of Kenneth Wilson Whitsett Papers, J. Murrey Atkins Library, University of North Carolina at Charlotte.

William Lawing, Faye's fourth great-grandfather, is believed to be the first Lawing to live in North Carolina. The family name seems to have evolved during the 1700s, with some early records of William's appearing with the surname Lewin and Lewing in addition to Lawing. Though there are no definitive records supporting when or where he was born, various family trees indicate he arrived in America from England; others record that he came from Germany. Based on oral family histories, William was most likely born before 1730 and living in North Carolina by the early 1750s. He married a widow, Jean

Killian Richards, in the late 1750s. Jean, who was of German descent, had two children, John and Elizabeth Richards, from her first marriage. Her father, Andreas (Andrew) Killian, came to America from Germany aboard the ship *Adventurer*, arriving in Pennsylvania in 1732. Several years later Killian and his family traveled south along the Great Philadelphia Wagon Road, settling beside the Catawba River in the 1740s in what is now Lincoln County.

One of the earliest records of William in Mecklenburg County is a 1763 land survey document that lists him as a chain bearer assisting with a survey for John Moore along the Long Creek watershed east of the Catawba River. In the following year William received a land grant of 125 acres in Mecklenburg County from the British governor of North Carolina. Following the Revolutionary War William received a second land grant for 150 acres on the waters of the Catawba River and Long Creek. He actively bought and sold tracts of land in the county through the end of the eighteenth century. The Mecklenburg County tax listings for 1806 is one of the last known records of his residence in North Carolina. Like many early North Carolina settlers, William appears to have grown weary of the growing population in the state and moved west. Lawing and Killian family histories indicate William, Jean, and several of their children left Mecklenburg in 1808 for Warren County, Tennessee. William lived at least until 1812, evidenced by the inclusion of his name on the Warren County tax listings for that year. There are no known dates of death for William or Jean, though it is presumed they died in Tennessee.

William and Jean had eight children (dates of birth are approximations and imply there could have been two sets of twins): Andrew, born in 1761, Elizabeth Susan (1766), William Jr. (1770), Jane and Mary Sallie (1775), Ann and David (1778), and Samuel (1782).

While William Lawing was settling in Mecklenburg in the 1760s, Daniel Caldwell, the first in Frank's family to live in America, was a young boy in Scotland. Born in 1754, he resided in the small parish of Southend, located in County Argyll on the Kintyre Peninsula. Living conditions in Scotland were harsh during this time; many struggled just to survive. Not surprisingly, thousands of Scots left their native country for a new life in America seeking greater religious freedom and better economic opportunities. A large number found their way to North Carolina, settling along the coastal plains and the Piedmont region. From 1773 to 1776, customs officials in England and Scotland compiled detailed records of emigrants leaving for America, documenting passenger names, ages, former residences, occupations, and reasons for emigration. A subset of those records documenting emigrants bound for North Carolina was compiled by A.R. Newsome and published in *The North Carolina Historical Review, volume 11, number 1,* in 1934. That compilation includes the list of passengers from Scotland on board the ship *Ulysses,* which sailed for Wilmington in North Carolina on August 12, 1774. Listed among the 93 passengers:

Dan'l Caldwell, 18, Kintyre, Shoemaker, Poverty Occasion'd by want of work.

If the age listed in the record is accurate, it implies Daniel was born in 1755 or 1756. Presumably, he was at least 19 when embarking on his journey, since his gravestone records his birth taking place in 1754. It surely took a great deal of courage for such a young man to embark upon a long journey to a new and unknown world far across the ocean. After arriving in Wilmington, Daniel made his way to Mecklenburg County where he settled and established a farm near the Rocky River Community. He served in the North Carolina militia during the Revolutionary War, taking part in the battle at Camden, South Carolina. In her notes on the Caldwell family written in 1915, Bettie Caldwell Woodruff, Daniel's great-granddaughter, included a short paragraph about his experience at Camden:

Daniel was down on his knees chipping his flint so it would spark the better. When he got up to fire, he found himself alone, and the British were so close he could see the colors of their uniforms. He soon, however, overtook his comrades and even passed them by.

The Battle of Camden was quickly lost that day with hundreds of Revolutionary soldiers and militia killed or captured. It was a disappointing setback for the Revolutionary forces, but fortunately Daniel survived the carnage.

In the 1780s Daniel married Mary Howie Greenlee, a widow from Kintyre, who emigrated with her husband, John Greenlee, on the same ship as Daniel. John apparently never made it to Wilmington, having died during the voyage. Daniel and Mary built a rock house in the Sugar Creek community and attended Sugar Creek Presbyterian Church. They had four children: Robert, born in 1787, Samuel (1788), James (1790), and Mary (1793). Daniel's wife passed away in 1825, and he followed two years later. They are both buried in the Sugar Creek Presbyterian Church Cemetery located along North Tryon Street in Charlotte, across the road from the church.

Daniel's brother, Robert, and sister, Barbara, also emigrated from Scotland and made their homes in Mecklenburg County. Another brother, John, along with his family, sailed from Scotland to America many years later. John died en route to the new country and was buried at sea. His widow, Jean, and their two sons arrived safely in America and joined their relatives in North Carolina.

Unlike William Lawing, Daniel was not the first Caldwell in North Carolina, or even Mecklenburg County, as other Caldwell families were living there long before he arrived. While it is possible some of those earlier Caldwell families may have been related to Daniel and his siblings, no definitive relations have ever been substantiated.

The Caldwell and Lawing families are among the oldest in the history of Mecklenburg County. Daniel and William lived during an exciting and difficult period when North Carolina and the other American colonies were fighting for their freedom. Mecklenburg County was in the thick of the conflict, proclaiming independence from England in 1775, a year before the Declaration of Independence was written, and defiantly resisting the invasion and occupation of Charlotte in 1780 by British General Lord Cornwallis. Daniel's and

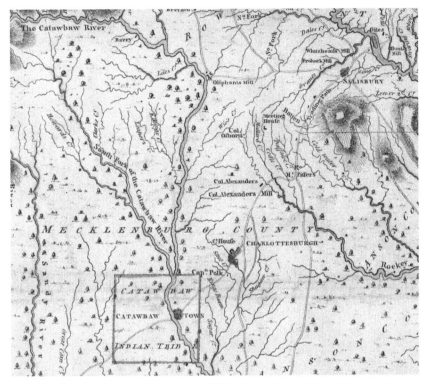

Mecklenburg County and the town of Charlottesburgh (Charlotte) as depicted in a map of Colonial NC published in 1770 for George III, King of Great Britain. Includes the Catawbaw (Catawba) River and the tract of land set aside for the Catawba Indian Tribe. Map courtesy of U.S. Library of Congress.

William's neighbors, friends, and fellow church members in the 1700s included the Alexander, Davidson, Torrence, and Knox families, many of whom are memorialized with streets, communities, schools, and colleges named in their honor.

In the more than 250 years following their arrival, thousands of Daniel's and William's descendants have lived in the Carolinas and throughout the United States. Many still call Mecklenburg County home.

Three

FARMING IS IN THE BLOOD

For the first 150 years of its history, Mecklenburg County was a rural area with most families scratching out a living from the land on small family farms. Starting with Daniel Caldwell in the 1770s, five generations of the Caldwell family were part of that farming community.

Early settlers like Daniel in the 1700s grew cotton, wheat, and corn while typically owning a mix of cows, hogs, mules, and chickens. Through the end of the eighteenth century, farmers primarily grew crops for their own use and consumption. There were no significant cash crops or organized markets, though crops were sometimes used to barter for finished goods. The introduction of the cotton gin, a device invented in 1793, which automated the process of separating the seeds from cotton balls, quickly changed farming in Mecklenburg County. By the early 1800s cotton had become a cash crop. Over time farmers devoted significantly more acres to cultivate cotton and, by 1850, the county was the third leading producer of cotton in North Carolina.

During this time Mecklenburg's leaders were ambitiously pursuing railroads to increase growth and prosperity in the region. In addition to improving transportation routes to and from the county, they envisioned shipping goods by rail rather than over land by horse and wagon, or by barge on the rivers. The Charlotte and South Carolina Railroad was the first to arrive, in 1852, followed by three more in the following eight years. The addition of the railroads made it much easier for local farmers to transport crops and reach new markets. Cotton and the railroads created a great deal of wealth for several local farmers who expanded their operations, owning large cotton plantations by 1860. Still, most county farms remained small, and the farmers poor, maintaining just enough livestock and crops to feed and clothe their families.

Mecklenburg County's agricultural growth was abruptly interrupted by the Civil War. Farmers traded their plows for guns and joined the Confederate army. In their absence the family farms were managed and maintained by women, children, and slaves. Following the war, small family farms rebounded quickly, with returning veterans planting and harvesting crops as they had years before. However, it was a dramatically different story for the former plantation owners who had relied primarily on slave labor.

Despite the demise of the plantations, cotton remained an important cash crop in the years following reconstruction. Advancements in cotton cultivation—primarily the use of a new fertilizer, Peruvian guano—greatly increased cotton yields per acre. With these improvements, even small farms of 100 acres or less could profit from growing cotton. And once again county leaders worked to rebuild and expand the railroads to transport cotton to market. Mecklenburg County's cotton production grew from only 6,112 bales in 1860 to 19,129 in 1880.

The county continued to be a major agricultural center in the early twentieth century with the number of farms and cotton production peaking in 1910. However, urban communities in Mecklenburg were growing even faster and, for the first time in that same year, the number of people living in towns and cities exceeded those living in rural

1880 - Mecklenburg County cotton gin and press. Photo courtesy of the Robinson-Spangler Carolina Room, Charlotte Mecklenburg Library.

1900 - Farmers bringing cotton to market in Charlotte. Photo courtesy of the Robinson-Spangler Carolina Room, Charlotte Mecklenburg Library.

areas; 34,000 of Mecklenburg's 67,000 population now lived in the city of Charlotte. The urbanization was attributable to the fast-growing textile industry and related businesses in Mecklenburg and surrounding counties. Powered by newly built hydroelectric plants, 300 cotton mills were operating within 100 miles of Charlotte by the early 1900s. With this rapid expansion, many farmers left the fields for jobs in the mills.

In the 1920s farming began to decline with cotton cultivation decreasing significantly due to higher costs and the pesky boll weevil. Cotton production in Mecklenburg would never regain its once lofty position, and the number of bales produced consistently declined over the next several decades. In the meantime, the county continued on a path of strong industrial and commercial growth, though this also displaced many farms in the community. By 1940 only 3,223 farms, a reduction of more than 25 percent from the peak of 1910, were in operation. Although agriculture remained viable for many more years, farming continued its steady decline following the end of World War II.

The Caldwell family had a long history of farming. Frank's third great-grandfather, Daniel, farmed in the Rocky River and Sugar Creek communities of Mecklenburg County, purchasing parcels of land and receiving small land grants from North Carolina. His holdings became substantial as evidenced by the county tax listings for 1811, which state he owned 585 acres. Based on the inventory of Daniel's estate recorded in Mecklenburg County shortly after his death in 1827, it appears Daniel had a comfortable life on his farm, better than the average farmer who only owned about 100 acres at the time. The inventory included, among other items, one horse, seven cows, 22 hogs, a wagon, three plows, two saddles, various farming tools, nine bushels of wheat, and two spinning wheels.

Daniel's son, James, was Frank's second great-grandfather. Born in 1790, he and his wife, Minty, owned a farm in north Mecklenburg County. They grew cotton, corn, and other grains along Clarke Creek near the Cabarrus County line. Mecklenburg County tax records indicate James owned 622 acres in 1815. Some of the land he cultivated near the old Concord Highway produces plants and flowers today. However, unlike 200 years ago, these plants and flowers grow in a massive complex of greenhouses owned by Metrolina Greenhouses.

Frank's great-grandfather, William Caldwell, born in 1820, was a highly regarded farmer, growing cotton, corn, wheat, and other crops on the same land his father farmed. He served as a captain in the Mecklenburg County Confederate militia during the Civil War and was often referred to as Captain William Caldwell after the war.

William and his wife, Angelina, purchased a 629-acre plantation in the historical Alexandriana community in the late 1860s. The property included a grand house named Rosedale that had three floors, a basement, a double gallery (porch) extending across the front, and four chimneys, each with three fireplaces. Guests arrived at the house via a lane lined with cedar trees, and this lane originated about a half-mile east of the property near the community post office and train station. It was one of the largest houses in Mecklenburg County, situated on property that was originally part of a much larger plantation

Rosedale, plantation home of William and Angelina Caldwell from the late 1860s until 1896. Photo courtesy of Kenneth Wilson Whitsett Papers, J. Murrey Atkins Library, University of North Carolina at Charlotte.

owned by John McKnitt Alexander, an influential Mecklenburg patriot during the colonial period. (Alexander was secretary of the county delegation that met in 1775 to draft the Mecklenburg Declaration of Independence, which preceded Thomas Jefferson's Declaration of Independence by more than a year. Alexander's grandson, Doctor Moses Winslow Alexander, the original owner of Rosedale, oversaw the construction of the house, which was completed in the 1840s.)

Over time William accumulated significant land holdings, at one point cultivating crops on more than 1,200 acres. Around 1885 he changed the Alexandriana post office and train station names to Croft in honor of his grandson, Croft Woodruff. William and his family lived at Rosedale for almost 30 years before selling the property in 1896. The Croft community still exists today, including two landmark structures, the old Croft schoolhouse and the S.W. and C.S. Davis General Store, both dating to the early 1900s. Sadly, after sitting vacant for many years, Rosedale burned in a fire set by vandals in 1967.

In addition to farming, William was a postmaster and community leader. His obituary in the June 15, 1901 edition of the *Charlotte Observer* read:

> *He was a farmer and a man of means, and was known and esteemed by practically everybody in the county. He was straightforward and honorable and had many friends.*

William's oldest son and Frank's grandfather, William Blake (WB) Caldwell, was born in 1860. He continued the farming tradition, living with his wife, Lenora, in Croft on property given to him by his father in 1882. Between 1904 and 1907, WB purchased four tracts of adjoining land in Mecklenburg County, including two parcels from his father-in-law, Isaac Frazier, creating a farm containing about 100 acres. During this time WB moved his family from Croft to the new farm located on Belt Road between Hoskins and Beatties Ford Road. The farm extended from current day North Hoskins Road south, just beyond the current Interstate 85 corridor. It was here that WB operated the Caldwell Sausage Farm, which was first started by his father-in-law.

By the time WB and Lenora moved to the farm, most, if not all, of their 11 children were born. Fortunately, the new farm had two houses to accommodate their large family. The larger house was one level, with three bedrooms, a porch extending across the front, three fireplaces, and a basement. Across the road and several hundred feet below the main house was a second, smaller home where some of the older boys in the family lived. The farm was in the country on a dusty dirt road, but it was reasonably close to urban areas—four miles from downtown Charlotte and just more than a mile from the Hoskins community.

WB and Lenora Caldwell (Frank's grandparents) family photo from about 1909. L-R Back: Thomas Parks (Frank's father), John Raymond, Angalene, Albert, Margaret. Front: Rebecca, Willard, Isabelle, WB, WB Jr., Lenora, Frazier, Mary.

Frank's father, Thomas (Tom) Parks Caldwell, was the second child born to WB and Lenora in 1889 on the family farm in Croft. Azalee Wilson, Frank's mother, was born in 1891 on a farm in Fort Mill, South Carolina, just across the state line. The oldest of four daughters born to Leander and Avalona Wilson, she also had an older half-sister, Margaret, from her father's first marriage. Azalee's parents died early in life: Avalona in 1900 and Leander in 1906. Afterward, Azalee and her sisters went to live with their uncle, Samuel "Pink" Wilson, his wife, Minnie, and their five children. Azalee was forever grateful to and very fond of her Uncle Pink. In the early 1900s she moved with her half-sister, Margaret, to Charlotte and lived at the local YWCA. She met Tom at the Belk Department Store where she worked in downtown Charlotte on East Trade Street. In 1913 Tom and Azalee married at her uncle's house in Fort Mill.

Like his ancestors, Tom was a farmer. He owned cows, hogs, and chickens on his small plot, which was part of the original hundred-acre farm owned by his parents. At some point early in their marriage, Tom and Azalee moved into the smaller house on his parents' farm, the same one he and his brothers lived in after the family moved from Croft. In 1919 Tom and Azalee purchased just more than two acres of land from his parents, which presumably included the house. Originally only one level, Tom added two upstairs bedrooms as his family grew. Tom and Azalee had three daughters and three sons: Sarah Elizabeth (Chuba) born in 1915, Lula (1917), Thomas Parks Jr. (TP) (1918), Frank (1920), Yates (1922), and Esther (1927).

WB passed away in 1923, leaving Tom and his brother, Albert, to operate the sausage business. Lenora continued to live on the farm with Albert until she died in 1943. With her passing, the farm was inherited by her eleven children, with each receiving a share of the land. By this time only Tom and Albert were living on the original farm; all of the other children were well established in non-farming jobs. Not surprisingly, on April 29, 1944, a year after Lenora's death, Albert purchased all of his siblings' shares of the farm. On the same day he sold

Wilson Family Photo from 1894. L-R Back: Lewis and Mary Ann (Frank's great grandparents), Theodocia. Front: Margaret, Azalee (Frank's mother), Leander (Frank's grandfather), Avalona (Frank's grandmother), Eva.

13 acres back to his brother, Tom, for the same price he paid for Tom's inherited share. After this transaction Tom owned about 15 acres of his father's original farm.

Frank's parents worked hard to make a living and provide for their family during difficult times, spanning the Great Depression and two world wars. In addition to being part owner of the sausage business, Tom also sold butter, milk, and eggs from his own farm to customers in the nearby neighborhoods of Hoskins and Thomasboro. He used his car for deliveries, removing the back seat to make room for the dairy products. Living on a farm was a plus in those lean times—at least there was food on the table. Tom and Azalee lived frugally, managing to send two of their daughters, Sarah Elizabeth and Lula, to Queens College in Charlotte during the depression years. Additionally, Tom bought a second car that TP and Frank shared when they were teenagers in the late 1930s. Those two boys must have been the envy of all their friends to have a car at such a young age.

Frank was the fourth child born to Tom and Azalee, arriving at the farm on October 9, 1920. Frank, TP, and Yates, having been born in a span of four years, spent a great deal of time together. While there were many chores to complete, the farm was a great place for kids growing up in the fresh country air. With few toys or material possessions, Frank and his siblings made their own fun. There were trees to climb, swimming holes along the creek, an abandoned rock quarry filled with water, and large pastures to explore. The boys' friends from the Hoskins and the Beatties Ford Road communities frequently joined in the fun on the Caldwell Farm. When not roaming the farm, Frank enjoyed pitching horseshoes and playing with homemade wagons and slingshots.

Tom and Azalee Caldwell's family in 1924. L-R Back: Lula, Azalee, Sarah Elizabeth. Front: T.P., Frank, Yates, Tom. Tom and Azalee's last child, Esther, was born later in 1927.

Life during Frank's childhood was not easy. Things taken for granted in today's world did not exist in his youth. There were no televisions, fast food restaurants, air-conditioning, kitchen appliances, or central heating. Families washed clothes by hand and hung them outside to dry on clotheslines. Outhouses, well water, coal-burning stoves, family gardens, and manual labor were the norms. At that time many rural homes in Mecklenburg County lacked electricity, running water, and telephones.

Money was scarce, so Frank's family improvised, using and repurposing almost everything they owned. Nothing was wasted; they saved and reused aluminum foil, bottles, wood, scraps of cloth, and the cloth sacks that contained feed for the hogs. Frank's mother, Azalee, stitched the scraps of cloth together in colorful patterns for quilts and used the cloth feed sacks as the backing for the finished product. A stash of used bottles and jars could always be found sitting on shelves in the garage waiting to be reused. Since his family did not have refrigeration during Frank's early childhood, a meal frequently required some advance planning, such as catching one of the family chickens, wringing its neck, chopping off the head, and plucking the feathers in preparation for evening supper.

Learning how to be self-sufficient was a necessity living on a farm in the first half of the twentieth century. Unlike today, where service providers are a call away, farmers had to depend on themselves to take care of their land, tools, livestock, and families. Farming was an extremely physical and

L-R: Frank and Yates on the Caldwell Farm in 1940.

manual process requiring long days of back-breaking work and as many hands as possible. Large farm families were the norm with the children toiling in the fields and maintaining the farms. From an early age, Frank plowed fields, fed the hogs, milked cows, gathered eggs, and harvested crops.

Frank and his siblings attended Long Creek School, catching the bus each morning for the seven-mile trip. The school, located on Beatties Ford Road, educated children from first grade through graduation. Like Frank, most of the students were from farm families in the northern part of Mecklenburg County. Interestingly, all four of Frank's sons attended the original Long Creek School for at least one year, though by then it was primarily an elementary school. The school still exists, but only two original buildings—the brick-clad gymnasium and concession stand, along with the rock grandstand by the baseball field—remain intact from the time Frank attended.

Frank graduated from high school in 1937 and, by that time, was already working in the family sausage business with his father and uncle. He was a happy young man, earning some money and enjoying life with his friends and brothers. Sadly, two years later, Frank and his family faced a terrible tragedy when the car driven by his brother TP was struck by a bus on Wilkinson Boulevard in Charlotte. Severely injured, TP only lived three days following the accident, passing away on September 24, 1939. He was 21. The Caldwell family was devastated by his sudden death, and Frank deeply saddened by the loss of his brother.

It is somewhat telling that only two of the eleven Caldwell children born to WB and Lenora, Tom and Albert, were farmers. Their siblings, like many other farming families, left the farm in search of jobs elsewhere. The exodus from the farms was for good reasons. Farming was a demanding proposition with modest financial rewards even during good economic times, and small farms could not support multiple families.

In the last few weeks of his life, Frank spoke of cultivating fields as a young man, using a wooden plow pulled by the family mule. He said the mule was stubborn, so he resorted to throwing dirt clods to get the mule to move. He was saddened somewhat by that memory, saying, "I shouldn't have done that to the poor ole' mule." He also recalled helping his dad deliver milk, eggs, and butter to his customers. Although Frank did not follow in his ancestors' footsteps and become a farmer, he learned a tremendous amount

1940 Portrait of Frank.

growing up on a farm. Those experiences and skills served him well throughout his life. There was always a bit of a farmer within Frank, and he had a strong attachment to the land where he was born, living his entire life on what was once the Caldwell Farm.

Four

LIFE IN THE MILL VILLAGE

The Lawing family lived off the land for many generations in Mecklenburg County. Faye's fourth great-grandfather, William Lawing, and his wife, Jean, farmed and accumulated multiple tracts of land along the Catawba River watershed in North Mecklenburg County during the 1700s. Numerous records of land transactions involving William can be found in the minutes of the Mecklenburg County Court of Common Pleas and Quarter Sessions from 1760–1810. William and Jean continued farming after moving to Tennessee around 1808.

William's son, and Faye's third great-grandfather, Andrew Lawing Sr., born in 1761, was a well-known farmer and community leader. Like his father, he acquired significant land holdings along the Catawba River in the Hopewell community of Mecklenburg County. He was appointed justice of the peace in 1807 by the governor of North Carolina, one of several justices presiding over the Court of Common Pleas and Quarter Sessions in Mecklenburg County. Andrew prospered as a farmer growing cotton and raising livestock on 800 acres of land. He also owned a canoe landing and fishery on the river. One of Andrew's neighbors was James Latta, a local merchant and owner of Latta Place, a two-story house built around 1800 on a plantation of

500 acres along the Catawba River. Latta Place, which has been preserved and is open to the public, lies about two miles from Hopewell Presbyterian Church.

At his death in 1825 Andrew's estate included 800 acres of land, two horses, six head of cattle, nine sheep, twenty hogs, a wagon, smith tools, a canoe, a cotton gin, a large supply of cotton, various farming tools, and household effects. Since Andrew died without a will, his children petitioned the court to divide his acreage into nine lots. The court approved the petition and also set aside property for his widow, Obedience. A hand-drawn map of the lots is included in the probate documents for Andrew's estate.

Andrew's son, Andrew Lawing Jr., was born in 1793 and was Faye's second great-grandfather. He served in the 1st Mecklenburg Regiment of the North Carolina Militia during the War of 1812, volunteering during the 1814 muster. Andrew Jr. and his wife, Elizabeth, farmed on the land inherited from his father in Mecklenburg County. Receiving one of nine lots from his father's estate, his farm was less than 100 acres.

John Middleton Lawing, Faye's great-grandfather, born in 1841, was the youngest of Andrew Jr.'s 11 children. By 1860, when his father passed away, John and several other Lawing family members had moved to Lincoln County. After serving in the Confederate army during the Civil War, John returned home to Catawba Springs, where he farmed until his death in 1907.

Charles Forney, Faye's grandfather, and John's oldest child, was born in 1861. He carried forward the farming tradition primarily in the small Catawba County town of Newton. By 1930, based on census data from that year, he had retired from farming. It was the end of the farming era for Faye's immediate family, as none of Forney's seven children followed in his footsteps. Instead, all found employment in the booming textile industry, working in the local cotton mills.

While farming was still dominant in Mecklenburg and neighboring counties at the end of the nineteenth century, the textile industry

Early 1900s postcard of four cotton mills in Charlotte. Photo courtesy of the Robinson-Spangler Carolina Room, Charlotte Mecklenburg Library.

was beginning to make its presence known. The industry leveraged its close proximity to the cotton fields and cheap, abundant labor and constructed numerous cotton mills from the late 1880s through 1920. To attract and retain employees, mill owners built neighborhoods of small homes alongside the mill facilities to house the workers and their families. Known as mill villages, these communities common-ly included stores, churches, schools, and recreation facilities. Many farmers, weary of crop failures, uncertain prices, and pests, gave up farming to work in the mills. While the promise of steady wages and cheap housing pulled farmers from the fields, they quickly discovered working in cotton mills presented its own set of issues. Those included long work shifts for meager wages and harsh working conditions in the dirty, noisy mills. Additionally, as had been the case on the farms, it was almost essential for the children to work in the mills as well to help support their families. By 1930 much of the textile industry had migrated from New England to the South, with the largest concentra-tion found in the Piedmont Carolinas.

As the twentieth century dawned, several members of the Lawing family moved off the farm to take jobs in the mills. Cora and Bertha Lawing, the two oldest children of Faye's grandfather, Forney, were employed at the local mill as cotton spoolers in 1900. The sisters were 17 and 13, respectively, and made no more than $5.00 to $6.00 a week based on average weekly wages for mill workers published in 1906. At this time there were no child labor laws, so it was not unusual to find very young children in the mills working 12-hour shifts, six days a week. Faye's father, Charlie Mack, followed his older sisters' lead, leaving the family farm to work in the local cotton mill. The earliest record of his employment is from the 1910 census, and it indicates that, at

Faye's parents, Charlie Mack and Carrie Lawing, in the early 1900s.

the age of 23, he worked as a comber, though he most assuredly was working several years earlier at a young age like his sisters.

Faye's parents, Charlie Mack Lawing and Carrie Blankenship, grew up in Catawba County and were married on October 19, 1907 in Newton. Once married, they moved to Lincoln County where their first three children were born: Arnold in 1908, Mae (1910), and Clifford (Peck) (1912). By 1914, Charlie Mack moved his family again, this time to Paw Creek in Mecklenburg County where he took a job at the recently built Thrift Cotton Mill.

Thrift Mill, named for the community where it was located, began operations in 1912 along the train tracks of the Piedmont and Northern (P&N) Railway several miles outside Charlotte. The mill's location in rural Mecklenburg County was unusual considering mills were typically built in heavily populated urban areas. The viability of the mill was, in part, made possible by the railway, which constructed a depot at Thrift about the same time the mill opened. This electric rail line ran from Charlotte to Gastonia, and it provided convenient transportation and rail services for the community and mill. The Thrift depot building, located at the intersection of Old Mount Holly Road and Moores Chapel Road, is the only P&N depot still standing in Mecklenburg County. Henry Kendall, a Boston businessman, purchased Thrift Mill in 1924, and he operated it under the name Kendall Mill until 1958. Although the last mill-related activities at the site took place in

Charlie Mack and children at Kendall Mill Village in 1936. L-R: Gene, Carl, Charlie Mack, Faye, Don.

the 1980s, the original brick-clad building and water towers are still intact.

After the family moved to Paw Creek, Carrie gave birth to seven more children. Florine (Flo) was born in 1914, Rosella (Rose) (1919), Loyah (Bud) (1921), Faye (1924), Gene (1926), and Carl (1929). Another daughter, born in 1916, only lived two months before dying from bronchial pneumonia and whooping cough. Mae, the oldest daughter, gave birth in 1929 to a son, Don Lawing, who grew up with the other children in the family. Shortly after the birth of her last child, Carl, Carrie underwent treatment for mental stress at the state hospital at Morganton, a psychiatric facility. Most likely she was suffering from postpartum depression, an illness that was not understood or diagnosed during the early 1900s. Unfortunately, once committed to the hospital, she was never the same. Although she eventually returned home, the responsibility for taking care of the younger children thereafter fell to Faye's father and her older siblings. Mae shouldered most of the load, serving as a mother figure for many of the younger children.

While Frank was growing up on a farm with no close neighbors, Faye spent her childhood in Kendall Mill Village, a self-sustaining community bustling with activity. The village had everything a family needed: community store, tennis court, scout cabin, horseshoe pitches, baseball diamond with a grandstand, even a nine-hole golf course. There were two community churches, Thrift Baptist and Thrift Methodist, as well as a small school across the street. Each summer the mill hired a youth coordinator to manage activities for all village children. Mill workers established accounts at the community store, which extended credit to the families until the workers received their weekly wages. The families typically settled their accounts on Friday when the mill employees were paid. The village was truly a place where mill families worked, played, and worshipped together.

Recreation and community activities were an important component of life in the village. Baseball was arguably the most important activity, and almost every cotton mill in the Carolinas sponsored teams. Having a competitive baseball team was so important that many mills competed for the most talented players, enticing them with choice jobs and pay incentives. Some of those baseball players were talented enough to later play in the major leagues. These included Hoyt Wilhelm, Whitey Lockman, and Pete Whisenant. Like other mills, Kendall fielded a baseball team for many years, providing uniforms and equipment for the players and hosting games at the village baseball diamond. Game days were big events with large crowds and a band playing in the adjacent bandstand.

Charlie Mack, Carrie, and their nine children and grandson lived in one of the larger mill homes at 708 Poplar Street. As one might imagine, space was a luxury in a house with 12 people. Built as a three-bedroom home, the family converted the sitting room into an additional bedroom. Even so, it is hard to imagine how 12 family members found a place to sleep! Faye recalled, as a young child, sleeping together with her three sisters in one bed. The family lived a simple life with few frills, but they always had the essentials: clothes, food, and a roof over their heads. While the family did not own a car, they lived close to the

Faye's fifth grade photo from 1935.

Faye's eighth grade photo from 1938.

Thrift P&N depot which provided access to Charlotte, Belmont, and Gastonia. The one luxury they did possess was a large radio built into a wooden cabinet that stood about four feet high.

Faye, the third youngest child in the Lawing household, enjoyed life in the mill village playing with the other children and developing close friendships that lasted her entire life. She attended the mill school for grades one through three and joined her older siblings at nearby Paw Creek School for the remainder of her education. The school, which no longer exists, was located beside Paw Creek Presbyterian Church on Mount Holly Road, about a mile from the mill village.

Providing for a large family during the Great Depression was a challenge. Faye's father toiled long hours working in the hot, noisy mill for modest wages. In 1939, the last full year Charlie Mack worked at Kendall Mill, the average weekly wage for North Carolina cotton mill employees was $13.40, according to data collected by the U.S. Department of Labor. To make ends meet, Faye's parents found other ways to increase their income and feed the family. Despite their already crowded living conditions, they occasionally took in boarders. Charlie Mack also bought and slaughtered a couple of hogs each year, housing them in a pen close by the mill. As the Lawing children grew older, several took on jobs to help support the household. Mae, the oldest daughter, only attended school through fifth grade; she then left to work in the mill. By 1930 three children—Mae, Peck,

Faye with friends at Kendall Mill Village in 1940. L-R: Jean Lippard, Faye, Frances Lippard.

and Flo—had jobs at the mill, while Arnold, the oldest, was employed at the local grocery store.

Faye's youth revolved around school, hanging out with girlfriends, and attending church functions at Thrift Baptist. Additionally, she played second base and centerfield on the Kendall Mill girls softball team. Faye often recalled traveling with her church to Ridgecrest, the State Baptist Church Conference Center located in the Western North Carolina Mountains. Although she enjoyed being with her friends, Faye was extremely close to her family, frequently getting homesick when away.

A loving father to all his children, Charlie Mack especially doted on Faye, his youngest daughter, who in his eyes did no wrong. Faye loved her father deeply and often shared memories of him with her children and grandchildren. Though money was tight, he generously gave her a small amount to ride the P&N Railway into Charlotte to attend movies with her friends. At the time, the cost for a round-trip ticket was less than a quarter, and a large bag of candy at the theatre cost a nickel. Sadly, Charlie Mack passed away on January 17, 1940, shortly before Faye turned 16. He was only 52 and left behind a widow with five children and a grandson still living at home. As was the norm in 1940, the older members of the family pitched in and cared for their siblings during this difficult time. Mae and Bud, the two oldest children at home, worked to support Carrie and the family financially. Another sister, Flo, frequently provided food from her husband's grocery store in neighboring Gaston County. When Bud joined the U.S. Navy in 1942, Mae became the primary provider for the family.

Faye with her sisters at Kendall Mill Village in the early 1940s. L-R: Faye, Rose, Flo, Mae.

The Kendall Mill water towers still stand today, overlooking the old P&N Railway tracks.

In September 1940, one year short of graduating from high school, Faye left the mill village to marry Frank. Her new home on the Caldwell farm would prove to be very different for the young girl from Kendall Mill. Over the years Faye frequently returned to her childhood home, visiting family and friends who continued to live and work there.

Carl Lawing, Faye's youngest brother, recalled life in the mill village: "People thought cotton mills were dirty, but Kendall Mill was the nicest place to work and had the nicest people in the world. We always felt safe and never locked our doors. The mill was a wonderful place and provided everything we needed." While life was good, he did acknowledge that, "Folks living in the mill village were rather poor." Though poor from a financial standpoint, many former mill families fondly recall the richness of life and the strong community ties they enjoyed in the village.

The textile industry contributed significantly to Mecklenburg County's economy for much of the twentieth century, but by 1990 most of the local mills had closed; they could not compete with foreign textile companies which utilized very cheap labor. Fortunately, a large number of the original mill buildings in the county are intact and have been preserved for other uses, continuing to remind us of the significant impact those early mills had on the growth of Charlotte and Mecklenburg County.

The same cannot be said for the preservation of old family farms, as only a few operate today. The vast majority have been replaced by roads, neighborhoods, and commercial developments.

Five

LIVING IN THE STICKS

When Frank and Faye married, they had very little between the two of them—not much more than their clothes and a few personal belongings. They had little money and no place of their own. It is not known how much they thought about those issues, or if they ever discussed their marriage plans with anyone other than Frank's brother, Yates, who accompanied them when they eloped to York, South Carolina on September 5, 1940. They obviously made at least one plan: to fudge a bit on their ages (six and two years older than actual for Frank and Faye, respectively) before they went in front of the judge to be married. Presumably, anyone under the age of 18 needed parental consent, though it was common for young teenagers to marry in 1940. E. Gettys Nunn, Judge of Probate for York County, performed the ceremony and signed the marriage license, which states Frank was 25 and Faye 18 years and five months. Nothing like being exact!

At the time of their marriage, Frank was working as a butcher at his Uncle Albert's sausage farm in addition to delivering blocks of ice for an ice house in Hoskins. Refrigerators and freezers were rare at this time, so blocks of ice were delivered to homes and businesses and stored in wooden iceboxes. Per 1940 census records, Frank's annual salary in 1939 was $600 a year, or about $11.50 a week.

Not having enough money to set up housekeeping, Frank and Faye moved in with his family on the Caldwell Farm. They made their first home in a small two-story wooden structure located only a few feet behind Tom and Azalee's house, setting up residence in the two rooms on the top level. It was a small, non-descript space without a toilet or bath, though it did have electricity and a single sink with running water. Below their home was the wash house; this was appropriately named since this level was where all of the Caldwell family bathed and washed their clothes. Bathing is a bit of an overstatement since it consisted of washing with a bar of homemade soap and a cloth using a basin of water. With no indoor bathroom, they used an outhouse that sat at the end of a cement walkway below their home.

Moving in with the in-laws was a lot to ask of a young girl of 16 who left her friends and family in the mill village for life on a farm. When describing her move to the Caldwell Farm, Faye stated, "It was

Early 1940s - Tom and Azalee Caldwell's farmhouse on Belt Road in Mecklenburg County. Behind and to the left of the house is the small two-story wooden building where Frank and Faye lived after eloping to York.

in the middle of nowhere, and I thought I had moved to the sticks." Considering where Faye lived as a child, "the sticks" was a reasonable description. Tom and Azalee's farmhouse sat on a small hill by a gravel drive about a hundred yards from the dirt road running by the farm. The road was simply called Belt Road between Hoskins and Beatties Ford Road. There were woods on both sides of the house, with fields and more woods in back. The only neighbors—Frank's grandmother, Lenora, and his uncle, Albert—lived together in the original farmhouse just up the road. At night a deep darkness fell over the countryside and it seemed a world removed from the laughter, bustle, and streetlights of Kendall Mill Village.

Tom and Azalee's two-story farmhouse was large for the times, with four bedrooms, a formal living room, small kitchen, dining room, and a scullery along the back of the house that included storage for blocks of ice and a pantry. A large porch extended across the front of the house. Tom and Azalee heated their home with coal, burning it in a pot-bellied stove in the dining room on the first floor. Like the small

1913 postcard depicting the water tower and mill village houses in the Hoskins community. Photo courtesy of the Robinson-Spangler Carolina Room, Charlotte Mecklenburg Library.

structure Frank and Faye lived in, there was electricity and running water, but no bathroom facilities. By the house, on the right side, was a garage with an attached lean-to where coal was stored. The farmyard extended along a path running below the garage and had a chicken coop, hog pen, and barn. The livestock on the farm included milk cows, hogs, chickens, and a mule. Their property, though small, generated a significant amount of food for the family: eggs, milk, chicken, pork, and vegetables. Azalee was an excellent cook, known for her fried chicken, homemade biscuits, and chicken dumplings. She kept her pantry well stocked with canned vegetables, soup mixtures, and jams. She was also a talented seamstress who made her own clothes.

Hoskins Mill Village was the closest community to the farm, about a mile away. The village, located along Rozzelles Ferry Road, contained a drug store, small grocer, and service station. Always busy with activity, the Hoskins Drug Store was a community institution with a pharmacy, soda fountain, and local post office. The Caldwell family frequently visited the post office to pick up their mail, addressed to: Hoskins Station, Box 283, Charlotte, NC. The service station, owned and operated by Mutt Cox, sold gasoline and serviced automobiles for several decades. Running parallel to Rozzelles Ferry Road, the P&N Railway had a stop at Hoskins Station just below the drug store. The railway continued about three miles beyond Hoskins and terminated in downtown Charlotte.

As 1941 drew to a close, Frank and Faye had been married for just more than a year. In that first year Faye felt a bit isolated and lonely, missing her family and the mill village activities. In addition to the change in scenery, it was difficult adjusting to a different lifestyle and the Caldwell family dynamics. Frank's father was a stern man; he had a command and control mentality that set a tone for his household and created some awkward moments. Adapting to life in her new home in Tom and Azalee's backyard was challenging. Fortunately, she became good friends with her young sister-in-law, Esther, and grew fond of Azalee, who taught her how to cook and sew. Those relation-

*Frank and Faye with
Frank's sisters at
the Caldwell farm
in the early 1940s.
L-R: Sarah Elizabeth
(Chuba), Lula, Frank,
Faye, Esther.*

ships, along with visits to her former home in the mill village, helped
Faye navigate a trying year.

On December 7, 1941 the Japanese bombed the U.S. Pacific naval
base at Pearl Harbor, Hawaii. The inevitable had happened, and the
U.S. was immediately at war. Shortly after war was declared, Frank and
his brother, Yates, like most able-bodied men, volunteered for military
service, with the U.S. Navy. Yates enlisted and served during the war,
but Frank was turned down because he had a history of kidney stones.
The Navy was concerned that he could not be medically treated if he
had a kidney stone attack while serving overseas. Faye's brother, Bud,
also volunteered to serve in the Navy, enlisting about the same time.
Frank was somewhat disappointed that he could not enlist, but Faye
breathed a sigh of relief that he was not going off to war.

World War II dominated all aspects of life at home and abroad.
It was routine to see military personnel in Charlotte. The city's municipal airport was converted into an army air base, renamed Morris
Field, and used to house and train pilots. Over time Frank and Faye,
like most everyone, came to know of friends, family, or neighbors
killed or wounded in the war. The young couple watched news reels

Christmas card Faye received from her brother, Bud, in 1943. The card depicts the ship Bud served on during World War II, the USS PC 562.

from the front lines in Europe and the Pacific at the movie theatres. They closely followed reports of every battle, troop movement, and campaign thoroughly covered by local newspapers and radio stations. As the war raged and battles continued across the oceans, there were significant efforts on the home front to support the effort. Sugar, flour, butter, gasoline, cigarettes, alcohol, metals, and many other foods and commodities were rationed among the population to assure the military had all the food, armaments, equipment, and support needed to win the war. Though money was scarce, citizens were encouraged to buy war bonds to financially support the war efforts.

Frank and Faye continued living in their modest accommodations on the farm, and Frank remained employed at the family sausage farm as the war dragged on. They lived frugally, scrimping and saving as much money as possible. People today would find it difficult to live as Frank and Faye did in the early years of their marriage. Frank once commented on those early days: "It was a hard life. We ate beans for supper almost every day. Young people today would not live like that."

Fortunately, Frank and Faye were accustomed to making do with what they had. Working on his father's farm from an early age, Frank was skilled in farming, hunting, and carpentry. He also was mechanically inclined. Faye proved to be a quick study of her mother-in-law's talents, learning to sew, cook, and manage a household. These experiences and skills proved invaluable as they awaited the next big event of their young marriage: the birth of their first son, Frank Jr., on May 10, 1943. Older, wiser, and now a new mother, the young mill village girl had adapted rather well to living in the sticks. With the addition of their firstborn, life was busier than ever, and their two-room home felt even smaller.

1944 - Frank and Faye with their first child, Frank Jr.

The war in Europe finally ended on May 8, 1945 after the Allies had crushed the German army and liberated the continent. Three months later the U.S. unleashed atomic bombs on both Hiroshima and Nagasaki, convincing Japan to surrender. World War II was officially over, and a weary country was jubilant. In the aftermath, the nation turned to the task of rebuilding the American economy. Military bases were dismantled, food staples and commodities gradually returned to normal levels, and most importantly, the soldiers returned home to a warm welcome from a grateful nation. Like all Americans, Frank and Faye were happy to see the war end and thankful their brothers, Yates and Bud, returned home safely.

Still hoping to build their own home, Frank and Faye were more focused than ever on assuring their family was financially secure and independent. They diligently managed their affairs, saving as much as possible and avoiding any debt. No matter how small his wages might be, Frank faithfully added to the family savings each payday.

After seven years of living with the Caldwell family, the young couple had finally saved enough to build their own house. On the morning of May 6, 1947, they traveled to the Mecklenburg County Courthouse in Charlotte to record the $50 purchase of just more than a one-half acre tract of land from Frank's parents.

With assistance from his father and Yates, Frank designed and built a sturdy house sitting on a rise above his parents' home. In 1948 Frank, Faye, and their son happily moved into their new home "up the hill." It was a simple wooden framed house with four rooms that more than doubled the space they previously lived in. They were still living in the sticks, with the same dirt road winding by the front of their new home, but the young couple now had more privacy and some distance from the extended family. The new house stood directly across the road from the original Caldwell farmhouse and the sausage farm, making Frank's commute to work a short stroll from the front door.

Within a year of moving into their new home, Faye gave birth to their second son, Tommy, on September 6, 1948. The family was growing, and it certainly was nice to be in a home they could call their own.

Six

THE GOOD LIFE

Following World War II, the new decade of the 1950s was a promising time of economic growth and prosperity in the United States. Soldiers returning from military duty after the war married their sweethearts and started families. The number of births skyrocketed and the children born in this period became known as the baby boomer generation. Businesses, schools, and housing throughout the U.S. expanded along with the country's population. Technology was advancing as well, with telephones, televisions, and electric appliances becoming common in homes. Baseball was the national pastime and television brought the games into people's homes on fuzzy black and white screens. Elvis Presley was an overnight sensation as he danced and crooned his way into the heart of every young girl in America.

Mecklenburg County and Charlotte expanded significantly with new businesses, roads, stores, and factories. The city's population in 1950 was just short of 135,000 as Charlotte continued to expand into the surrounding county. Though there were still a number of farms located in the county, more and more people were employed in manufacturing jobs, many of which supported the textile industry. At the same time new industries, an expansion of banking services, and improved transportation corridors were beginning to shape Charlotte's future.

As farming waned in Mecklenburg County, many farmers sold parcels of land to family members, resulting in small communities of closely related families, some of which still exist as of this writing. Such was the case for Tom and Azalee, as over time they sold tracts of land or provided housing to most of their children, creating a small Caldwell family community living on property that was once part of their farm. In addition to Frank and Faye, Yates and his wife, Edith, Esther and her husband, Jack Correll, and Chuba and her husband, Earn Bartlett, lived nearby.

While the world was rapidly changing at the start of the decade, life around Frank and Faye's home remained much the same. Frank continued to work for his uncle at the Caldwell Sausage Farm while Faye focused on her growing family and managing the household. The dirt road still wound its way by Frank and Faye's home, and the surrounding area remained rural, with farms extending along the dirt road in both directions. According to Faye, she still lived in "the sticks," and many years would pass before Frank would purchase that first television for the family.

Lula Demarest with Frank Jr. standing by the Stewart Creek bridge along the dirt Belt Road between Hoskins and Beatties Ford Road in 1946.

When he was not working, Frank kept busy growing a garden, raising his own hogs, and doing chores around the house. His carpentry skills were put to good use as he built a standalone garage using wood salvaged from an abandoned tenant house on the farm. He also added a small smokehouse at the edge of his property, called the green house for its green-colored siding. Every year late in the fall when the weather turned cold, Frank would slaughter and butcher a hog, hanging the hams to cure inside the smokehouse.

Like his father and grandfather, Frank had an interest in farming and hoped to acquire more property to pursue his dream of owning his own small farm. He approached his Uncle Albert and asked him to sell the property adjacent to his own, but Albert refused to part with the additional land, though he did later sell about a half-acre to Frank and Faye in 1953.

There was not much time for relaxing as Frank was driven to financially provide for his family. He and Faye continued their thrifty way of life while being careful to use their limited resources wisely. Frank only received one week of vacation each year, and in the interest of making additional money for his family, he filled in as a butcher for a small grocery store located in Hoskins during his vacation week. While many friends and family were quick to buy the latest appliances, televisions, and new cars, Frank and Faye resisted the urge to spend and lived well within their means.

A young mother of two boys, Faye stayed busy taking care of Frank Jr. and Tommy. She was the consummate homemaker, keeping her home spotless, washing baseboards, mopping floors, and dusting every nook and cranny. With Frank working across the street, Faye prepared three cooked meals every day for her family. She also spent considerable time doing the laundry and hanging clothes to dry on the backyard clothesline. During her free time Faye played with the boys, perfected her seamstress skills, and took on small sewing projects for friends

Frank and Faye with their sons, Frank Jr. and Tommy, in 1949.

and family. When Frank Jr. started school, she volunteered as a grade mother helping with school functions and attending Parent Teacher Association meetings.

Frank and Faye's third son, Dan, was born on June 4, 1952. It seemed a pattern had emerged: Faye was having another baby about the time her youngest child was getting ready to start school. On October 31, 1957, five years after Dan was born and within a year of when he would be going to school, she gave birth to her fourth and final son, Myron. Frank's siblings were also adding to their families. Yates and his wife Edith had four children, Barbara, Wayne, Larry, and Gary. Frank's sister Esther and her husband Jack Correll had four as well, Harvey, Donna, Jackie, and Marcia.

Sundays in the 1950s were devoted to family and church with Frank, Faye, and the boys attending McGee Presbyterian Church in the morning and then spending the afternoon with the extended Caldwell or Lawing families. Invitations to visit were not necessary as it was generally understood and expected that family would gather at

Frank and Faye in 1953.

the homes of the grandparents. After all, most socializing took place in the home, and people looked forward to company dropping in.

Frank and Faye often visited Faye's mother at her home in Kendall Mill Village on Sunday afternoons after church. Her mother continued to live there with her oldest daughter, Mae, for about 20 years following her husband's death. Most of Faye's siblings and their families lived in close proximity to Carrie in Paw Creek or just over the Catawba River in Gaston County. An extremely close-knit family, on any given Sunday several family members gathered at the Lawing home, typically congregating on Carrie's front porch.

Frank, Faye, and the boys also spent many Sunday afternoons with the extended Caldwell family at Tom and Azalee's house. It was not unusual to have a gathering as large as 20 family members. During warmer weather the adults sat on the front porch catching up on local news and a bit of gossip while the kids played. Baseball was by far the game of choice and always took place in the large front yard of the house. Worn bare spots served as the bases and the outfield extended up a hill across the graveled driveway that passed in front of the house. Jack Correll helped the kids build a makeshift pitcher's mound and backstop in the front yard. Sometimes baseballs would hit the front porch of the house, sending the adults scurrying for cover. More than once, a window fell victim to a hard line drive, shattering the glass panes. Amazingly, no one seemed to get too excited about it, and Frank typically repaired the broken panes.

The kids who were too young for baseball played the "rock game" on the steps leading to the porch. This was a game of chance to see who could get to the top step first, with the participants guessing which hand of the person conducting the game contained a rock. It was a simple game that kept the little ones entertained. As the afternoon turned into evening and darkness began to settle in, the kids chased lightning bugs, capturing them in empty mayonnaise jars, played tag, or watched for the first star to appear in the night sky. Eventually everyone returned home for the night. For most, that involved a short walk to their nearby houses.

The 1950s were a happy time for Frank and Faye as life on the farm was simple and uncomplicated. While the boys were getting older, they were still young enough to not have many cares or worries. The quiet countryside around the farm conveyed a peaceful existence, though it was frequently interrupted by the laughter of the Caldwell cousins playing along the creek in the woods or their moms yelling for them to get home for dinner.

The farm felt safe, and no one worried about formalities or locking doors.

There were sad times as well. Faye's oldest brother, Arnold, committed suicide in 1956, and later that year, Frank's father, Tom, suffered a fatal heart attack at the age of 67. These sudden deaths were unexpected and a shock to the Lawing and Caldwell families. In 1958 Uncle Albert retired and closed the family sausage business. That same year he sold 34 acres of the farm to Atlantic Terminals and Warehouses Incorporated, which then built a trucking terminal for Johnson Motor Lines. One-third of the original farm was no longer owned by the

Dan, Tommy, Myron in 1959.

Caldwell family, and more land sales would follow in the next several years.

With the closing of the sausage business, Frank accepted a new job working at a sawmill for the McClure Timber Company in Paw

Creek. By the end of the decade some improvements were clearly visible around the Caldwell home. The dirt road was paved and had a new name: North Hoskins Avenue (later changed to North Hoskins Road). Frank made an addition to the house, adding a new kitchen, dining area, and enlarging the front porch. Rural route mail deliveries were expanded to include direct delivery to Frank and Faye's house.

And Frank eventually bought a television, which became a highly appreciated source of entertainment for the entire family.

Seven

CALDWELL'S SAUSAGE

The Caldwell family sausage business had a profound impact on the first half of Frank's life. Growing up on the Caldwell farm, Frank became familiar with the business at an early age, observing his father and uncle managing and operating the enterprise. At 16, he joined the family business, though he also held additional jobs in those early years. In the 1940s he began making sausage full time and enjoyed a long career at the company, conveniently located across the street from his home.

Caldwell's Sausage was well known in Mecklenburg County, dating back to the early 1900s, near the turn of the century, when Frank's great-grandfather, Isaac Frazier, started a part-time business in the basement of his farmhouse. Having a few extra hogs on hand, Isaac made pure country pork sausage, selling it to nearby individuals and a few local businesses, including the Stonewall Café in downtown Charlotte. The cafe, located across the road from the Southern Railway station, proved to be a fortuitous customer, serving the sausage to railroad employees who took a liking to the food.

Within two years, Isaac's part-time sausage business had evolved into a full-time operation. He signed a contract with Southern Railway to supply their dining cars with his sausage. Southern was a large enterprise, carrying passengers to major cities along the southern seaboard from Florida to Washington, D.C. Transitioning from a part-time business to one requiring a steady supply of hogs and continuous sausage production was more than Isaac could handle on his own. Frank's grandfather, WB Caldwell, agreed to join the fledging business once the contract with Southern was finalized. It was the beginning of what would become a well-known enterprise that would produce and sell Caldwell's Sausage for almost 60 years.

1908 postcard of Southern Railway Terminal and Stonewall Hotel in Charlotte. The Stonewall Cafe, where railway employees discovered Isaac Frazier's sausage, was located in the hotel. Photo courtesy of the Robinson-Spangler Carolina Room, Charlotte Mecklenburg Library.

Although the railroad was by far the largest customer, WB and Isaac also sold sausage to individual customers, delivering it directly to their homes. Developing their own recipe, they made sausage using the whole hog and adding a special seasoning. The formula worked as word-of-mouth advertising from local customers, along with positive reviews from passengers dining on the Southern Railway, generated much interest. By the end of 1907, WB and his wife purchased Isaac's farm and became the sole owners and operators of Caldwell's Sausage.

WB carried on the small family business operating out of the same farmhouse basement. Hogs were sourced locally in Mecklenburg County and carefully selected to assure a high quality product. While some local farmers raised a small number of hogs and made home-made sausage for their own consumption, few considered starting a business to compete with Caldwell's. In fact, WB faced little to no competition while he owned and operated the business through the early 1920s. Still, it was a challenging operation, one requiring a great deal of manual labor and proper planning to assure the sausage was made fresh and delivered on time, especially to the railroad.

The notoriety of Caldwell's Sausage grew quickly. An article in the *Charlotte News* on March 6, 1914 featured a copy of a letter written to WB from a lady who had the pleasure of eating his sausage while traveling on a Southern Railway train between Washington and Jacksonville:

Feb. 13, 1914
Berlin, N.H.

W.B. Caldwell
Charlotte, N.C.

Dear Sir:

I had some of your family sausage on the Southern Railroad dining car between Washington and Jacksonville this winter and liked it so much that I asked where it came from. Your brother gave me your address. I would like you to send me 20 pounds by express to the following address. I am a Southerner and I miss the sausage up here in New England. Please send at once and mail your bill to:

Yours very truly,

Caroline Gordon Brown

The brother referred to in the letter was WB's younger brother, Thomas Edney Caldwell, who was employed by Southern Railway as a dining car conductor on the Charlotte to Jacksonville route.

Frank's father and uncle, Albert, took over the operation of the sausage business in 1923 after his grandfather, WB, passed away. The brothers operated under a new name, Caldwell Brothers Pure Pork Country Sausage. Albert and Tom followed the same business model established by their father and grandfather over the next two years, focusing on direct deliveries to local customers and the railway. In 1925, as many of their long-term customers were moving into the city and surrounding suburbs, Albert and Tom changed their sales strategy and began distributing their sausage through local stores rather than delivering directly to customer homes. The sausage was freshly made, wrapped in wax paper in one-pound packages labeled as Caldwell's Sausage, and delivered daily to the stores. The new marketing process worked as their sausage became a sought-after commodity and one regularly featured in local store advertisements in the *Charlotte Observer* and *Charlotte News* by Reid's Stores, Morris & Barnes, and S.R. Lentz among others.

Stores frequently featured Caldwell's Sausage in their newspaper advertisements. This ad was placed in The Charlotte Observer *on February 4, 1932.*

By 1930 two more local sausage producers, Wilson's Sausage in nearby Huntersville, and Morrison's Sausage in south Mecklenburg County, entered the Charlotte market. With the addition of these businesses and the growing demand for sausage, it became difficult to find enough high quality hogs in the county. Seeking to remedy this issue, Albert met with local farmers, encouraging them to raise more hogs to meet the growing needs. The farmers responded positively, and by the early 1930s Caldwell Brothers Pure Pork Country Sausage was buying 400 hogs a year. Considering an average hog weighed 200 to 250 pounds, and about 50 percent of a hog's weight was used in making sausage, the brothers were producing 40,000 to 50,000 pounds of sausage annually.

Frank became the fourth generation of his family to make sausage when he joined the business in 1936. Four years later Albert took over sole ownership, buying out Tom and changing the name to Caldwell's Farm Sausage Company. Business was brisk in the 1940s, and demand for Caldwell's Sausage on Southern Railway's dining cars grew to 300 to 400 pounds a day during the World War II years. Meeting Southern's daily needs while also continuing to supply local retail stores kept the small business fully engaged.

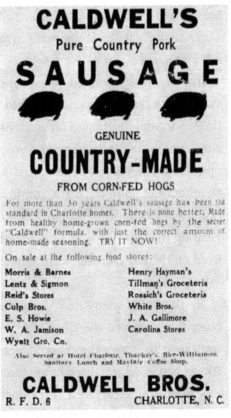

Tom and Albert placed their own advertisements for Caldwell Brothers Sausage in The Charlotte Observer, *including this one from November 26, 1933.*

During Frank's employment there were usually four individuals, including Albert, working in the company. For many of those years the other two employees were Frank's brother, Yates, and Johnny McMurray. Albert supervised the work with Frank and Yates doing the most labor intensive tasks, and Johnny usually making the daily deliveries. A typical day started early in the morning with a truck arriving from the local abattoir delivering dressed hog carcasses to the farmhouse basement. The carcasses were deboned, meat removed, processed through a motor-powered grinder, and laid out on a large wooden table. After mixing the ground meat with the special family seasoning of salt, imported sage, and red and black pepper, the sausage was weighed and manually wrapped with a Caldwell's Sausage label attached.

The business operated year-round, though the days of operation varied between seasons, usually Monday through Friday and sometimes Saturday in the winter months, with a shorter schedule in the summer months. Albert's wife, Elma, played an important part in the operation, ringing a bell mounted just outside the side door of the farmhouse at noon to let the employees know it was lunch time, and doing so once more at five o'clock to signal the end of the work day. Hearing the bell ring was a big treat for all the Caldwell cousins who lived on the old Caldwell farm. They affectionately came to call Elma "Aunt Ding Ding."

By the 1950s many new competitors, mostly large meat packing companies, entered the Charlotte market as the demand for sausage continued to grow. The marketplace had evolved significantly since Albert began selling directly to stores some 25 years earlier when he was only competing with three packing house brands. During this same period Southern Railway's daily requirements for sausage decreased to only 150 pounds, less than half the demand during World War II. The lower demand from the railroad meant more sausage sales had to be allocated to local grocery stores. The additional competition for shelf space in the local grocers kept sausage prices low and put pressure on profit margins.

Albert decided to end operations in 1958. He was 60 years old and had been managing the business for the past 35 years. When asked shortly after closing why he stopped making sausage, Albert responded, "I cannot make enough money." Caldwell's Sausage operated for almost 60 years through two world wars, a great depression, and the post-world war economic boom, making sausage in the same small basement of the farmhouse on

James Albert Caldwell, about 1930, owner and operator of Caldwell's Sausage.

North Hoskins Avenue. Whether it was the growing competition, financial pressure, or just the right time to end the business, the company had a remarkable run, and Charlotte lost a treasured institution.

Having worked in the family business for 22 years, Frank was saddened to see the company close. He moved on to a new job, but for a long time he missed the sound of the bell ringing each workday at noon and five o'clock.

Eight

SPARE THE ROD, SPOIL THE CHILD

Growing up under the watchful eye of their parents, the four Caldwell boys quickly learned right from wrong and the rules they were expected to live by. Frank and Faye taught them to play nicely, share, respect the property of others, and to address adults as ma'am and sir. Frank was strict and a firm believer in the biblically based principle "spare the rod and spoil the child." The Caldwell boys learned that Frank was good as his word and certainly did not spare the rod or, in his case, the belt, when warranted. He also deployed another technique to quell unruly behavior, popping the top of the guilty son's head with his knuckle. This most frequently occurred during church services. With his long arms he had an uncanny ability to reach down the church pew and "knock a knot" on the deviant's head if he was misbehaving. The boys learned sitting as far as possible down the pew from their dad might spare them a pop on the head.

Likewise, Faye had high expectations of her boys and was willing and able to dole out discipline as needed. Her preferred tool was a switch, typically taken from the forsythia bush at the side of the house, which proved to be extremely effective on bare legs. Faye also believed in the power of words, frequently delivering well-scripted speeches to the boys when going somewhere to visit or shop. The key points included basic rules such as: "Don't touch anything," "Stay with me and hold my hand," "Don't go wandering off," and "If you break something, you will have to pay for it." These admonishments typically worked well with the boys, especially after testing the rules and suffering the consequences.

If there was one rule that Faye held sacred, it was her stipulation that the boys stay in the yard and not leave the property without her permission. This was one of the most difficult of the rules for the boys to obey because there were always places to go, things to do, and lots of cousins to do them with. And after all, as was often said, "the cousins were always free to come and go whenever they wanted." Of course, Faye had given this stipulation much thought over the years and had good reasons for instituting the rule. To put this in perspective, imagine 100 acres of rural land with creeks, wooded areas, an abandoned rock quarry, farm animals, and barns. Add to that mix twelve grandchildren, most owning pocketknives and slingshots by the time they were six years old.

What may have influenced this seemingly harsh rule? A number of events over time involving Frank Jr., Tommy, Dan, Myron, and their cousins. Perhaps it first came to mind when, at the urging of Frank Jr., Tommy, who was only four or five, took his pocketknife and stabbed his cousin Barbara, in the arm. One would have expected Frank Jr., five years older than Tommy, to have known better than to suggest such a thing. Fortunately, the knife did not break through skin and no blood was shed. Unfortunately, Tommy's exploits continued to factor into the need for the rule along with, shortly after the knife incident, Tommy breaking his wrist after falling off a wooden platform. By the way, older brother Frank Jr. was with him at this incident. Was a pattern emerging?

Two of the cousins, Wayne and Harvey, who were nicknamed "the lab doctors" by their uncle, Earn Bartlett, contributed to Faye's con-

*The five oldest Caldwell family cousins. L-R: Harvey Correll,
Wayne, Barbara, Frank Jr., and Tommy Caldwell.*

cerns. The boys liked collecting bugs and small animals and conducting "experiments." The two were frequent partners in crime, once getting caught by their grandfather throwing rocks at his barn windows. Wayne, well known for collecting tobacco from his dad's cigarette butts and rolling his own using old newspapers, preferred the colored comic section from the Sunday editions. He explained to his cousins the colored paper tasted better than black and white! Harvey, on the other hand, was the mad scientist of the group, fascinated by animals and bugs. One of his claims to fame was digging up a recently buried dead dog. His reason was simple enough: he wanted to see what it looked like! Harvey liked snakes as well, catching a large black one and taking it to school for "show and tell."

However, the event that may have really sealed the deal for Faye's rule was the spike-throwing episode. Having stumbled upon a pile of long steel spikes near Johnson Motor Lines, Tommy, Dan, and some of the Caldwell cousins happily took the spikes back home to their grandmother's pasture for fun and games. Everyone was having a grand time throwing the spikes into the ground until Tommy—who else?—threw one through his foot. Frank Jr. was not present this time, but he was summoned to carry Tommy home with the spike still in his foot.

After visiting the doctor to have the spike removed, Tommy was on the mend and ready for future adventures. Of course, he did not disappoint, as he later managed to break his other wrist, proving once and for all that it does not pay to swing from one tree limb to another. Obviously, Tommy, like many other boys, enjoyed playing with sharp objects and undertaking death-defying feats.

*L-R: Tommy, Barbara, and Frank Jr. before Tommy's
many adventures and mishaps.*

Interestingly, it appears Frank Jr. was frequently involved in the activities that spurred Faye's restrictive nature. Seldom the perpetrator of the actual deed, but often the instigator, this oldest of the four encouraged his brothers—and cousins—to partake in questionable behaviors. Most likely he enjoyed getting them into trouble, as evidenced by his suggestion that Tommy and his cousin, Larry, shoot rocks with their slingshots at Aunt Lula's car. Responding to Frank Jr.'s thought-provoking idea, Larry proved his excellent marksmanship as a young boy of five, launching a rock from his slingshot directly into her car. He scored extra points since she was driving while he executed the shot! Needless to say, Lula was not happy.

Faye's younger sons, Dan and Myron, also contributed to the reinforcement of and need for her rule. Dan's turn in the spotlight took place when he was only two years old and supposedly in the care of his oldest brother, Frank Jr. One would believe Frank Jr. was old enough to have learned his lesson from past mistakes and keep a watchful eye on his little brother. However, that was not to be, as on this particular day Dan wandered off from home and was lost for several hours. Panicked, the entire family looked high and low. Fortunately, George Watts, a neighbor, who lived and worked on Uncle Albert's farm, found Dan deep in the woods. Of course no one can really blame a two-year-old kid for such a mishap, so Frank Jr. suffered the consequences and still recalls the whipping he received that fateful day. Dan did have his own moments as the years passed, including the time he crashed into the water when trying to walk on the frozen creek.

1960 - Caldwell family cousins. L-R: Harvey, Wayne, Barbara, Dan, Tommy, and Larry. Myron in front.

Certainly, justification for the rule was further strengthened when Faye's youngest son, Myron, at the age of five, walked behind his cousin Harvey, as he was throwing up rocks and hitting them with a baseball bat. Not paying attention, he walked directly into Harvey's backswing, which caught him square in the forehead, sending blood flowing down his face. The blow left a visible scar at the hairline on his forehead, at least while he still had hair.

Based on all this, Faye's rule seemed to be well justified. The boys usually obeyed. However, the temptation to cross the line was always present, as was the irresistible opportunity to get one another in trouble. In the latter case, Tommy was usually the instigator, coaxing and telling Dan all would be well if he left the yard. To this day Tommy delights in recalling Dan's misfortune when Faye realized he had left the premises, and his own good fortune at being able to journey beyond the yard with his mom when she went to bring Dan home. While it was entertaining to Tommy, it was not a happy outcome for Dan.

1964 - Myron's first grade picture. The telltale scar from the baseball bat incident is clearly visible along his hairline.

Despite Faye's stringent rule, the four boys were actually given quite a bit of latitude to explore and play. They grew up in the clean air and open spaces of the Caldwell farm, most often roaming Uncle Albert's land. On most any day they were not in school, the boys could be found playing outside. In fact, on Saturdays it was not unusual for them to be out of the house early in the morning, only to return for lunch and dinner.

The farm was their playground where they went on long walks, explored the woods and pastures, and fished in the creek. They picked blackberries, gathered wild hickory nuts, and ate green apples until their stomachs ached.

While Frank and Faye were busy working and managing a household, they also took time out to have fun with their sons. They sometimes accompanied them on the farm, walking on the well-worn paths created decades before that snaked through the woods and along the pastures and creek. There was something special about this property; it was easy to become attached to the pull of this land. For the four brothers it was an opportunity to share many of the same experiences as had their father and grandfather, exploring and playing on the property.

There were a number of unique places on the Caldwell farm commonly known to the extended family. While these "landmarks" did not have any special notoriety outside the farm, they were noteworthy to, and a natural playground for, several generations of Caldwell kids. Over time some of those places acquired names that were passed down through the years. The gravel drive extending from North Hoskins Road, turning in front of Tom and Azalee's house and curving up a steep grade, led to the Big Hill. The Big Hill was one of the highest elevations on the farm, located just below Frank and Faye's house. Here the Caldwell grandchildren spent hours playing hopscotch and marbles, digging in the dirt, and swinging on a rope swing in the cool shade of the giant oak tree that towered over the hill.

Stewart Creek crossed a large swath of the farm extending through woods and along pastures where cows and horses grazed. The outer edge of the pastures, down by the creek, were cooler in the summer and contained some of the best wild blackberry briars in the area. Fences of barbed wire stretching across posts made from cedar trees kept the livestock in place. A great deal of time was spent in Stewart Creek building dams, fishing, and playing. Landmarks along the creek included the Elbow and the Catfish Hole. The Elbow was named for the shape of a turn in the creek similar to a human elbow. The Catfish Hole was a favorite fishing spot, though it did typically yield more crawdads than fish. The Big Rock, adjacent to the creek, rose about 15 feet in the air and was a favorite for climbing.

A gravel road running through the woods on the farm behind Uncle Albert's house led to an old quarry where rock was once mined. It was abandoned in the early 1900s and subsequently filled with water from an underground spring. The quarry had a sheer rock face running along one full side that rose about 25 feet above the water line. Frank told the boys stories of kids jumping off the rock wall into the water when he was a young boy. The quarry was known as the Rock Hole and was a popular swimming and fishing destination for generations of Caldwells and their friends.

Living in a simpler time, the world moved slowly and life was centered around family and making your own fun. It was hard to beat the walks in the woods, wading in the creek, and simply exploring the great outdoors. For Frank and Faye, as well as their four boys, these were the best of days.

Nine

CHANGING TIMES

By 1960 Mecklenburg County and Charlotte were experiencing explosive growth with the city's population exceeding 200,000. Manufacturing, textiles, banking, transportation, and wholesale distribution were instrumental in bringing additional investment and new jobs to the county. Charlotte was becoming a destination city attracting patrons from throughout the Carolinas to attend shows, concerts, and sporting events at the Charlotte Coliseum and Ovens

Aerial view of Charlotte's growing downtown in the 1960s.
Photo courtesy of City of Charlotte Corporate Communications.

Auditorium complex. The city was home to two local television stations, WBTV and WSOC, along with eight radio stations and two daily newspapers. With the world rapidly innovating and changing, the stage appeared set for an exciting and prosperous decade ahead.

In 1960 Frank and Faye celebrated 20 years of marriage. Looking back, they were thankful for the life they shared, their four sons, and the home they built together. Frank was employed in a relatively new job at McClure Timber Company while Faye was content keeping house and looking after the four boys. It was a good life, but the quiet and simple years of the prior decade were giving way to a more complex and challenging period for Frank and Faye. The boys were growing up and the nearby community was dramatically changing. Frank Jr., the oldest, was in his final year of high school and looking forward to attending college. In a short period of time most of the farms along the former dirt road were sold to developers, making way for warehouses and businesses.

Uncle Albert, now retired, rented his barn and pastures to others to house their livestock. He also continued to sell off portions of his farm, including four acres to Emerson Newton, who built a machine shop on the property beside Frank and Faye's home. A few years later Albert sold an additional 40-acre tract to the Spangler Land Company, and that land was subsequently developed into a large neighborhood by the Ervin Construction Company. With the sale of most of the farm complete, the local landscape looked very different as neighborhoods and businesses were fast encroaching on the peace and serenity of North Hoskins Road. At night it was still dark, but a smattering of lights could be seen through the woods in the new neighborhood. While more than 35 acres of the farm still existed, things did not feel as safe and secure as before.

As they often do, events happen fast and without warning. So it was in the summer of 1961 when a fire destroyed the McClure Timber Company sawmill where Frank was employed. Overnight the sawmill disappeared along with Frank's job. Though the company provided

Frank with another job grading lumber, he left shortly afterward for a new opportunity, accepting a job at Dixie Electric Motor Repair Company. He enthusiastically dove into his new line of work studying at night and on weekends to become a licensed electrician. The work was often difficult and some projects required working overtime, but Frank never complained about the long hours or strenuous work. In fact, he enjoyed the challenges and the opportunity to work extra hours to increase his earnings. Little did he know at the time this was the beginning of his second career working as an electrician—one that would span almost 40 years.

Celebrating Frank Jr.'s graduation from high school in 1961. L-R: Faye, Dan, Frank Jr., Myron, Tommy.

A great deal of activity took place in the Caldwell family in the 1960s. Frank Jr. worked at the A&P on West Trade Street while in high school, saving money to pay his way through college, since Frank and Faye did not have the funds to pay for a college education. He entered Brevard College in 1961 and completed his studies there during the next two years. In 1964 the youngest Caldwell son, Myron, entered first grade at Long Creek Elementary School. That same year Tommy and Dan, the middle sons, were entering the eleventh and seventh grades, and Frank Jr. was taking a break from college and working at Celanese Corporation. A few years later Frank Jr. completed his college education and accepted his first position as a teacher, in Greenville, S.C. As Frank's mother, Azalee, grew older, her health began to falter. No longer able to care for herself without assistance, Frank and his siblings made the difficult decision to place her in a nursing home in 1968.

Easter, 1964. L-R: Tommy, Myron, Dan.

During these times Faye was busier than ever running the household, fixing meals, taking care of her family, and helping the boys grow up. It was a challenging time with so many things going on in her life. As usual, she put others before herself, and her health suffered for it. Eventually she had to be hospitalized to treat an ulcer, but fortunately she made a full recovery.

The decade of the 1960s was a trying period not only for Frank and Faye, but also for the U.S. Violent riots in major cities, the assassinations of President Kennedy, Robert Kennedy, and Martin Luther King Jr., along with rising crime rates, stole America's innocence. The Civil Rights Movement highlighted, painfully, the inequalities and unfair treatment of minorities in the country. Popular music, protests on college campuses, and the hippie generation challenged traditional norms in American culture. And the one event that ignited more issues than any other was the Vietnam War. It was a war the U.S. could not win, a war that divided a nation, and one that was broadcast on television into America's living rooms every evening.

As the war escalated, hundreds of thousands of young men were drafted to serve in the controversial and unpopular war, including Tommy, who received his draft notice in early 1968 at the age of 19. After going through basic and advanced training at Fort Bragg and Fort Gordon, respectively, he received orders to report to Vietnam.

The greatest fear parents can imagine settled in for Frank and Faye when Tommy left on an airplane that fall for a one-year tour of duty. Frank and Faye prayed continuously, wrote letters, and sent care packages throughout the year. They diligently watched the *CBS Evening News* with Walter Cronkite, eagerly listening for updates about a war raging on the other side of the world in a small Southeast Asian country.

Looking back, the 1960s was a decade of unprecedented change in America and the world which would have long-lasting impacts for years to come. It was a decade that produced a lot of great music and the successful Apollo space program, which culminated with the safe landing of an American man, Neil Armstrong, on the moon in July 1969. However, it was also a decade filled with turmoil and a great deal of uncertainty. For Frank and Faye it was a period that, at times, felt like the world was turning upside down.

The Caldwell Family, Christmas 1969, shortly after Tommy returned home from Vietnam. L-R: Frank, Faye, Myron, Frank Jr., Tommy, Dan.

Nevertheless, the decade ended on a happy note for the Caldwells when Tommy returned safely home from Vietnam in the fall of 1969.

By 1971 Frank and his siblings had exhausted most of Azalee's limited resources to pay for her medical and nursing home bills. With those costs continuing to increase, Frank and his siblings decided to sell her home and its surrounding 14 acres to fund her medical care. Soon after the sale, the farmhouse, barn, and wash house were demolished and the surrounding land flattened. Not long after that

The Caldwell farmhouse, photographed in 1968, was last owned by Uncle Albert. The family sausage business, beginning with Frank's great-grandfather, Isaac Frazier, operated out of the basement of the house for about 60 years.

Uncle Albert's health took a turn for the worse, and he was admitted to a nursing home as well, passing away in December 1972 after a brief stay. His house, most likely a hundred years old or older, was in reasonably good condition and remained empty for about a year following his death. Unfortunately, vandals set fire to it, causing so much damage that it was subsequently burned in a controlled fire training exercise conducted by the local fire department. The last 22 acres of the original Caldwell farm left in Albert's estate were later sold at auction, but they sat dormant for many years, becoming so overgrown that any prior evidence of a farm simply vanished.

Unfortunately, the turmoil and unrest from the 1960s carried forward into the 1970s as well. Confronted with a multitude of serious issues, this was a gloomy period in U.S. history. The country's stature was severely compromised at home and abroad by the failed war in Vietnam. Economic woes followed when Arab countries in the Middle East imposed an oil embargo on the U.S., creating gas shortages and doubling prices at the pump. Remarkably, Mecklenburg County and Charlotte fared better than many areas of the country, continuing to expand and attract an influx of new businesses and residents throughout the decade.

As the Arab oil embargo took hold in 1973, Frank and Faye took their turns waiting in long lines to purchase gas. Throughout the decade they experienced the economic pinch of escalating prices for groceries, fuel, electricity, clothes, and other basic needs. While the annual inflation rate eventually rose above 10 percent, Frank's wage increases were much smaller, in the low single digits. Inflation, rising unemployment, and an uncertain future took its toll on the U.S., leaving Americans financially stressed and bewildered. The financial woes led to the development of a new economic indicator known as the "misery index," which was calculated by combining the inflation and unemployment rates.

To make matters worse, Frank's health took a hit in 1971 when he incurred a serious back injury that eventually required surgery. To his disappointment, the surgery did not completely eliminate the pain, and, in fact, damaged nerves in his left leg. Physically, he was never the same, as over time his left leg weakened further, leaving him with a noticeable limp and frequent pain. Undaunted, Frank managed through this setback and continued working for nearly 30 more years.

The 20 years comprising the decades of the 1960s and 1970s were likely the most difficult and challenging for Frank and Faye. Bolstered by a strong marriage, faith in God, and a loving family, they managed through those trying times. They lived well within their means and also found time to celebrate the good times: special family events and milestones. By the early 1970s the three oldest sons were married and starting their own families.

Without a doubt, some of Frank and Faye's happiest moments, and a renewed, positive outlook on life, came during that decade with the births of their first six grandchildren: Danita, born in 1973, Jennifer (1974), Carrie and Andrew (1977), and Amanda and Chad (1979).

Ten

KEEPING THE FAITH

Throughout their lives, Frank and Faye exemplified biblical principles and an unwavering faith in God. Christianity was the cornerstone upon which they lived and the basis for their family morals and values. Like most of their generation born and raised in the South, much of their lives revolved around church. In addition to being a place of worship, churches served as a focal point for social, educational, and entertainment activities.

Reflecting its rich Scotch Irish history, Mecklenburg County is home to a large number of Presbyterian churches. Attracted by a significant population of Scotch settlers, early Presbyterian ministers began arriving in the backwoods of North Carolina in the 1740s and 1750s. Over the next three decades they helped organize Presbyterian churches in and around Mecklenburg County prior to the American Revolution. Among these were the "Seven Sisters": Sugar Creek, Hopewell, Providence, Centre, Rocky River, Poplar Tent, and Steel Creek. The churches brought a sense of order to the wilderness and provided a centralized gathering place for worship, social activities, and discussion of local issues. Several early ministers were outspoken champions of the American Revolution, urging their congregations to rebel against the tyranny of British rule. Two hundred and

Hopewell Presbyterian Church, founded in 1762, still holds services on Beatties Ford Road in Huntersville. Faye's third great-grandparents, Andrew and Obedience Lawing, and Frank's great-grandparents, William and Angelina Caldwell, attended Hopewell.

fifty years later, these churches still stand as a testament to the faith of these early Presbyterian pioneers. All were in service when Frank and Faye's forefathers, William Lawing and Daniel Caldwell, lived in Mecklenburg County. Over time, many of their descendants attended these churches.

The Caldwell family was rooted in the Presbyterian tradition starting with Daniel, who attended Southend Presbyterian Church in Scotland before leaving for America. He and his wife, Mary, were members of Sugar Creek Presbyterian Church and are buried in the cemetery facing North Tryon Street in Charlotte. Daniel's son and Frank's second great-grandfather, James, was a member of Ramah Presbyterian Church. The earliest existing church records at Ramah date to 1838 and include James as a ruling elder. He and his wife, Minty, are buried in the cemetery on Ramah Road in Huntersville, across the street from the church. William and Angelina, Frank's great-grandparents, also attended Ramah before moving their membership to Hopewell

Ramah Presbyterian Church, established in 1783, is located on Ramah Road in Huntersville. Frank's second great-grandparents, James and Minty Caldwell, were members and are buried in the church cemetery.

Presbyterian Church in the late 1800s. William served as an elder at both. Frank's grandparents, WB and Lenora, were long-time members of Williams Memorial Presbyterian Church on Beatties Ford Road; WB was church superintendent and an elder. Frank's parents also attended Williams Memorial and, later, McGee Presbyterian Church in the nearby Hoskins community. Several Caldwell family members, including Frank's parents and grandparents, are buried in the Williams Memorial cemetery.

Faye always spoke proudly of the Lawing family's Baptist heritage and how much she enjoyed attending Thrift Baptist Church as a young girl. In fact, she was adamant that Baptists are better singers, better preachers, and most certainly the friendliest Christian denomination. Faye may have been surprised to know her family actually had Presbyterian roots! Her third great-grandfather, Andrew Sr., and her second great-grandfather, Andrew Jr., were members of Hopewell Presbyterian Church. Andrew Sr. is buried in the church's historical cemetery. Over time the Lawing family did affiliate with the Baptist Church, as first evidenced by Faye's great-grandparents, John Middleton and Elizabeth Lawing, who attended Mountain View Baptist Church in Catawba County, North Carolina. Charles Forney and Dovie Lawing, Faye's grandparents, were members of Lawing's Chapel Baptist Church in Maiden, North Carolina.

Thrift Baptist Church in Kendall Mill Village was situated across the street from the mill, only a short walk from the Lawing home. It was built on a plot of land donated by Thrift Mill and held its first service in 1914. Faye's mother, Carrie, attended that first service and was a charter member of the new church. While the mill also generously donated $500 to assist with the building, the fledging congregation had a need for additional funds for furnishings and supplies. Using their resources wisely, the congregation initially sat on benches made of wooden planks placed atop empty nail kegs. Carrie, along with two other ladies, Blanche Mauney and Bessie Beatty, served as Thrift Baptist's first fundraising committee. During the early days of the church, the three of them rode on the P&N Railway to neighboring Gaston County, where they visited with local textile executives and solicited funds. Carrie remained an active member for the rest of her life, faithfully attending until her death in 1972.

1938 - Faye with friends from Thrift Baptist Church at Ridgecrest Baptist Conference Center in the North Carolina mountains. L-R: Faye Spradly, Annie Lee Broome, Faye Lawing, Etta Wright.

If given a choice, Faye would have remained a Baptist, but that was not to be the case as Frank and Faye continued the Caldwell family's 200-plus-year Presbyterian heritage.

On Sundays the Caldwell family went to church. That was the rule, and there were no exceptions unless someone was near death. A typical Sunday morning at Frank and Faye's house began with southern gospel music on the television while the boys dressed in their Sunday best. Shoes polished, clothes on, and hair combed, the family piled into the car for the short ride to McGee Presbyterian Church, a small congregation organized in 1913 in the Hoskins community, just over a mile from the Caldwell home.

McGee's wooden frame building was constructed in a classic country style similar to those found in many southern communities. It was painted white and had several red brick steps leading up to a recessed front entrance. A small churchyard, framed by a short stone wall, stood beneath several tall trees. Just inside the front door of the church was the vestibule with an old woven rope hanging from the belfry connected to the church bell. Beyond the vestibule were three sections of whitewashed pews separated by two aisles leading to a raised pulpit and choir loft at the front. On the back side of the sanctuary was another smaller, wooden-framed structure known as The Hut, which was used for church offices, pot luck meals, and various church functions.

Being a small community church, McGee's members knew each other well; most grew up together in or near the Hoskins community. In many ways McGee was similar to the church depicted in the fictional TV town of Mayberry, N.C. on the *Andy Griffith Show* from the 1960s. Prior to the service, several men of the church, wearing their finest suits and felt hats, stood outside in the churchyard discussing the topics of the day. Every Sunday morning at 10:45 A.M. the church bell rang signaling the service was about to begin. There were elderly ladies sitting in the pews wearing black hats, children squirming in their seats, a choir (more often than not singing off key), and church members occasionally dozing during the service. Whether on key or

Sketch of McGee Presbyterian Church, organized in 1913 in the Hoskins community of Charlotte.

not, the congregation as a whole sang boldly and out loud, making a joyful noise. Though, according to Faye, not as loud or as well as her former Baptist church.

Frank and Faye's family was large enough to fill an entire pew. Although church members did not have assigned seats, everyone knew the Caldwell family sat in the back pew on the left side. Similarly, most other long-term members tended to sit in the same spot every Sunday. At times it was a little awkward, but comical as well, when visitors would dare sit in someone's pew. Even today, former members can recall where specific families chose to sit during the services. Observing all the activities and commotion from the back pew of the church was frequently humorous to the boys, who often had difficulty controlling their giggles and laughter. That is typically when the long arm of Frank would reach down the pew and pop the boys on the back of the head with his knuckle.

Frank and Faye were active members at McGee, generously supporting the church financially and also contributing their time and talents. If the church door was open, it was almost a certainty the two of them, along with their family, were present. Frank and Faye were well respected as faithful workers and leaders and involved in almost every aspect of church life. For many years Frank served as Sunday School superintendent directing the assembly of church members before the Sunday School hour each week. In particular, he enjoyed leading the members in singing before they were dismissed for classes. He loved the old gospel hymns and could always be heard above others belting out the words to his long-time favorites like "Blessed Assurance," "Amazing Grace," and "How Great Thou Art." As an indication of their faith in Frank's leadership, church members elected him to serve as a deacon or elder multiple times. In 1958 he had the honor of working as a counselor at the Billy Graham Crusade that was held in the original Charlotte Coliseum.

Faye too was a dedicated church worker, serving as a youth Sunday School teacher with her good friend, Dot Kiestler, while also helping in the children's nursery. She adored children, enjoyed teaching them the Bible, and listened attentively to their stories each Sunday morning. Faye also participated in the women of the church circle meetings and volunteered for Christmas pageants, Vacation Bible School, covered dish dinners, and Halloween carnivals. Her reputation as an excellent cook was well established in the church, and not surprisingly her ham biscuits were a big hit at covered dish dinners, quickly disappearing.

Frank dressed in his Sunday best in 1957: suit, felt hat, and well shined shoes.

Even in the last few years of her life, Faye was still supporting her church, baking coconut pies for the annual bake sale.

All of the Caldwell boys attended McGee into their teens. The church was like a second family, and the boys obtained a strong Christian foundation from the Bible stories, songs, and church activities. McGee was where they learned stories of faith, made their first friends, acquired social skills, and developed an understanding of community and belonging.

By the time McGee celebrated its 80th anniversary in 1993, it was struggling to stay viable. Many older members had passed away or moved from the local community, and membership had steadily declined for several years. McGee eventually shuttered its operations in the late 1990s. The congregation sold the church property and merged with two other struggling churches on Charlotte's west side. The combined congregations established and built a church in the Oakdale community, Pleasant Grove Presbyterian. Frank and Faye moved with the congregation to the new church and remained members there the rest of their lives.

The former McGee Presbyterian church building still stands today, and it looks much as it did when the church was first built more than a hundred years ago. It is now a funeral home on John McCarrol Avenue, just a block off Rozzelles Ferry Road in the Hoskins community.

Eleven

HAPPIER DAYS

Following the despair and setbacks of the prior two decades, the 1980s ushered in a happier and more peaceful period for the U.S. There were no major wars, there was a reduction in crime, and the decade also brought a renewed pride in America. A former actor from California, Ronald Reagan, was elected President in 1980 largely by promising America's future was brighter than ever. While it took several years, by 1984 that promise was coming to fruition as inflation and interest rates had declined, the U.S. economy expanded, and the overall mood in the country turned positive once more. Through the end of the century new technologies ex-

Charlotte's ever changing skyline in the early 1990s, including the recently completed 60-story Nationsbank (now Bank of America) Building on the far right. Photo courtesy of City of Charlotte Corporate Communications.

ploded on the scene, including personal computers, cell phones, and the Internet. The quality of life for most Americans improved, making those 20 years some of the most prosperous of the twentieth century.

Once more, Mecklenburg County grew tremendously in this time, with Charlotte emerging as one of the largest cities in the country. The city's slogan from 1940, "Watch Charlotte Grow," was still appropriate six decades later with the city boasting a new airport, several major bank headquarters, and professional sports franchises in the NBA, the Charlotte Hornets, and the NFL, the Carolina Panthers. Uptown was significantly transformed with new apartments, office buildings, entertainment venues, and businesses. The county's textile mills and farming communities, which dominated during the early years of Frank and Faye's lives, were practically nonexistent by the dawn of the twenty-first century.

During these happier days, four more grandchildren arrived: Tyler, born in 1986, Heather (1987), and Shannon and Katie (1989), giving Frank and Faye a total of ten. Affectionately known as MawMaw and PawPaw, the progression from parent to grandparent was remarkably transformative for both, as these two strict adults suddenly became pushovers. No matter what their grandchildren said or did, they could do no wrong in the eyes of their MawMaw and PawPaw.

When the grandchildren came to visit, they were Faye's top priority, and she gave them her full attention. Physically getting down on their level, she played games, read books, and catered to their every need. Not one to listen very well to the wishes of the parents, like any good grandmother she spoiled her grandchildren with ice cream, cookies, and toys. When she realized she may have overdone it, Faye would take the children aside and say, "Don't tell your parents we did this." Her instructions typically fell on deaf ears as the grandchildren were always bursting to tell their parents the wonderful things they did with their grandmother. At the end of a visit with MawMaw and PawPaw, Faye would reveal a stash of candy she stockpiled in a chest of drawers, encouraging her grandchildren: "Fill your pockets and take all you want." And why not? A little extra sugar never hurt anyone!

Faye especially enjoyed having her grandchildren stay overnight. This provided opportunities to take them to church, visit family members, and spoil them rotten, as she liked to say. The grandchildren eagerly anticipated the overnight visits to MawMaw's house since they usually included an outing to McDonald's, shopping at the dollar store, and visiting the petting zoo at Hornet's Nest Park. Faye loved to show pictures of her grandchildren to family and friends, always carrying a small brag book in her purse with the most recent photos. As she revealed her pictures Faye would typically share a couple of comments. First and foremost, every grandchild was "the prettiest baby I have ever seen." She also liked to point out the color of their eyes, exclaiming, "Look at those brown eyes. Now that is a Caldwell baby!"

Frank was just as enamored with his grandchildren. One would never have guessed he was once the rigid disciplinarian who adhered to the adage of spare the rod, spoil the child. He was all in with spoiling them and, in particular, enjoyed the hugs and kisses from his granddaughters. That tough grandfather was putty in his grandchildren's hands.

Faye with her four youngest grandchildren in 1998. L-R: Tyler, Heather, Faye, Katie, Shannon.

Continuing a tradition dating back to their childhoods, Frank and Faye extended a standing invitation to their sons' families to gather with them on Sundays for a cooked lunch. Rising early on Sunday mornings, Faye prepared a large family meal, usually cooking a roast in the oven while at the Sunday church service. By lunchtime the table in the dining area along with the bar in the kitchen were covered with dishes of food. Family members sat throughout the house eating Faye's home cooking and drinking sweet ice tea. It was a boisterous and happy scene at the Caldwell home with as many as twenty family members in attendance. The conversations were loud and lively with the four sons and Frank frequently talking over each other. The food was excellent and plentiful, and no one went home hungry after leaving Faye's lunch table.

Frank and Faye also hosted annual Easter, Thanksgiving, and Christmas holiday celebrations for the extended family. Faye was an extraordinary cook who insisted on preparing all the food for these gatherings, often baking days before the celebration. She laid out an impressive array of choices: turkey, stuffing, ham, macaroni and cheese, country style steak, sweet potato casseroles, creamed potatoes, potato salad, deviled eggs, and fruit salads. Her desserts were legendary: delicious pound cakes, pecan, coconut, and chocolate meringue pies, chocolate marshmallow cakes, brownies, and many others. She thoughtfully made special dishes for the grandchildren on these occasions and sent leftovers home with them. Christmas was Faye's favorite holiday. She baked cookies, stocked up on candy, bought and wrapped presents, and decorated the house before everyone arrived to celebrate. The Caldwell Christmas celebration was chaotic with wrapping paper, toys, and boxes flying everywhere in the crowded living room. These holiday traditions at the Caldwell home continued until Frank and Faye were nearly 80 years old.

In 1990 Frank and Faye celebrated their 50th wedding anniversary with a party hosted by their sons and daughters-in-law at the Coulwood Community Center in West Charlotte. All ten of their

Frank and Faye celebrating their 50th anniversary in 1990.

grandchildren were in attendance for the festivities. This milestone was recorded in a brief news article that appeared in the local newspaper, *The Charlotte Observer.* The story included the secret to their long marriage: love, respect, and faith in God. They also shared their recipe for rearing children: "To give lots of love, to be patient, and to bring them up in the church." While they received many gifts at the celebration, Frank and Faye would always agree the best gift they received was the fellowship of their family.

The years of living within their means and saving for the future gave Frank and Faye more financial security in their later years. Still, Frank continued to work for most of that time, because, simply put, that is what Frank enjoyed doing: having a purpose and providing for his family. Faye also had a part-time job, working at the polls for Mecklenburg County when elections were held. The job was seasonal and only required a few days of her time each year. In his later years Frank still found fulfillment in his job, but he also took more time to enjoy life, traveling (by car) with Faye to Niagara Falls, New Orleans, Charleston, Disney World, the Appalachian Mountains, Maine, and many other places.

In 1993, Frank encountered two new health issues, a heart attack and diagnosis of early stage prostate cancer. While recovering from the heart attack, the company where he had been employed for more than 30 years, Dixie Electric Motor Company, informed him he no longer had a job.

Undeterred by those events, Frank was not ready to give up working even though he was 73. Within the same year, he took on a part-time electrician job, and this kept him happily employed well into the future.

Twelve

HUMBLE AND KIND

Like many others of their generation, Frank and Faye had a strong work ethic and never shied away from a hard day's work. At home, church, or on the job, both carried out tasks with a methodical precision. Frank was a perfectionist who believed that if a job was worth doing, it should always be done right. He was not one to take shortcuts or rush through an activity. Faye was just as particular in all the things she did, including housework, sewing, cleaning, cooking, and caring for her children.

A devoted Christian and gentleman, Frank was humble and reserved. He was a homebody, one who enjoyed the solitude of life in the country. Serious and shy by nature, he was a man of few words, never seeking notoriety or an opportunity to promote himself. He disliked gossip, and it was extremely rare to hear him say anything critical or disparaging about anyone. He faithfully read his Bible, prayed to God, and was thankful for all the blessings bestowed upon him. A disciplined and principled individual who led by example, throughout his life Frank focused on doing what was right no matter the circumstances. And when he gave his word, he always followed through.

Frank never professed to be a model school student; he graduated from high school with average grades. However, he was a model student of life, learning practical skills and blessed with an abundance of common sense at an early age. He lived through periods of hardship and witnessed financial and personal struggles

1992 - Frank on the job with Dixie Electric at the age of 71.

during the Great Depression and World War II. The memories associated with the first few decades of his life shaped his character, instilling in him the desire to never be a burden to anyone and to financially provide for his family. From an early age, and until he died, he was laser focused on achieving financial independence and saving for a rainy day.

Work was Frank's vocation, one that brought him joy and gave him a purpose and sense of satisfaction throughout his life. Consistently employed for more than 60 years, his work ethic was hard to match. He enjoyed two very different careers: 22 years at the family sausage farm followed by almost 40 years working as an electrician. Though always slim, the many years of manual labor added a muscular tone to Frank's thin physique, and this was evident by the firm grip of his handshake. His scarred hands, often bruised and cut, revealed the physical toll of his work. While employed as a licensed electrician, he frequently climbed ladders, lifted heavy objects, and worked in attics and crawl spaces in extremely hot and cold conditions. Despite the physical nature of the jobs and the long hours, Frank was always thankful to be employed and embraced the tasks at hand. Every evening after returning home from work, sitting at the dinner table, he talked about his day and the people he encountered. The stories Frank told were a clear indication of how much joy he found in a good day's work.

A man of strong will and determination, Frank overcame physical challenges that would have derailed many others. In the last 30 years of his life he endured a great deal of pain from the back injury he suffered in his early fifties, but he did not let that issue become an obstacle. Never one to complain, he did not ask for any special disposition and went on with his life.

In contrast to Frank's reserved nature, Faye was an outgoing individual, a woman who thoroughly enjoyed being with friends and family, attending church events, sharing in small talk, and catching up on a bit of gossip. In truth, Frank never had to worry about talking as long as Faye was present; she could talk enough for both of them. She was a strong Christian and a loving caregiver, one who was always there for others, volunteering to help family or friends in need. Visiting shut-ins, keeping in contact with family members, preparing food for church functions, and taking relatives to medical appointments—all were common activities for Faye. Kindness was a way of life, and putting others before herself was second nature.

Faye was selfless when it came to her family, never taking a day off, even when not feeling well. She took great pride in caring for and nourishing her children and supporting Frank. When hosting family meals she made sure everyone was served and had full plates of food before serving herself. If the boys needed new clothes or supplies for school, Faye took care of that first before considering her own personal needs. She truly believed cleanliness was next to godliness, and she worked extremely hard to keep her house spotless. Family and friends were known to comment that her house was so clean you could eat off her floors!

Frank and Faye, Christmas 1998.

In addition to cleaning, two of Faye's other passions were cooking and sewing. She was an exceptional cook who seldom followed a recipe when preparing a meal, relying on memory and instinct instead. Her reputation as a cook spread beyond her family as friends and fellow church members had opportunities to enjoy her dishes at family reunions and church potluck dinners. Faye's interest in sewing turned into a lifelong hobby and a way to earn "spending money" by sewing for friends and family. She was so happy to welcome her daughters-in-law and granddaughters to the family, thrilled to have the opportunity to sew dresses and clothes for them. In her later years Faye made quilts for each grandchild using scraps of material she accumulated from sewing over many years. Those quilts remain treasured to this day.

Although Frank and Faye never attended college, both were well grounded in sound economic concepts and followed three simple financial principles throughout their lives. First, set aside and save a portion of every paycheck. Second, buy only what you truly need. And third, don't buy what you cannot afford. Disciplined in managing their financial affairs, they paid cash for purchases and avoided taking on debt. That financial philosophy worked well as they were able to build their own home by 1948, paying for it with cash they saved over the first seven years of their marriage. Skills developed and lessons learned early in their lives helped Frank and Faye stretch their lim-

The house that Frank built in the late 1940s. Faithfully adhering to their financial principles, Frank and Faye never had a mortgage on their home.

ited funds. Making do with what they had, they never strayed from their financial principles, always living within their means throughout their lives. Though money was sometimes tight, they provided a good living for their family, even if it was a simple one. There were few frills and extras, but the family always had plenty to eat and was well clothed, sheltered, and enjoyed all the basics of life.

Warmly welcoming visitors into their home, Frank and Faye enjoyed spending time with family and friends. Most visits involved lively conversation and food, with Faye offering cake, cookies, and other baked goodies to her guests. She loved feeding people, encouraging them to eat, and then to eat some more. Her sons' friends especially enjoyed stopping by knowing they would get to sample some of Faye's desserts. Not wanting visits to end, Faye would almost protest when her guests were leaving. Her typical comment was, "You just got here. What's your hurry?" That statement was always followed by, "Come back to see us!"

Perhaps the most telling traits exhibited by Frank and Faye were those which revealed how they treated and interacted with others. Those can be summed up in two words: humble and kind. As hard as they worked to make a living and care for their immediate family needs, Frank and Faye always found time to support their church, friends, and extended family. They believed in tithing and faithfully gave 10 percent or more of what Frank earned to their church. Additionally, they supported several charitable organizations, notably Barium Springs, a home for children in need, March of Dimes, Alexander Children's Home, and the Red Cross. Frank and Faye did this cheerfully and willingly even though it meant they had less for themselves. They were excellent role models, exhibiting these traits for their sons to see, and teaching them to be generous as well. When the boys were young, Frank gave them coins to put into the Sunday school offering at church. He also gave them a weekly allowance. Considering the modest wages Frank made throughout his life, never earning as much as $20,000 in any year he worked, he and Faye gave away a considerable amount of what they had to others.

Frank and Faye were extremely gracious individuals, content with their simple lifestyle and thankful for the many blessings they received. They cherished their faith in God, family, and friends more than any material possessions. Not expecting anything in return, their generosity and kindness came from the heart.

Thirteen

WHEN ALL IS SAID AND DONE

A new century arrived on January 1, 2000 with a great deal of fanfare and worldwide celebration. For Frank and Faye, it was just another day, but there were several significant milestones ahead in 2000, beginning with their 60th wedding anniversary on September 5. A month later, on October 9, Frank celebrated his 80th birthday. However, the most significant milestone of the year was Frank's decision to retire from working due to his physical limitations. Employed since he was 16 years old—64 years, something few people can say!—Frank struggled to fill his days with meaningful activity after retiring.

As the year 2000 came and went, the new century seemed poised for continued peace and prosperity. Sadly, that outlook was shattered on September 11, 2001 when a small group of terrorists launched several attacks on the U.S., including flying two airplanes into the World Trade Center twin towers in New York City. For several days the world stopped in its tracks. An anguished nation mourned its dead and anxiously waited to see if more attacks would follow. Like all Americans, Frank and Faye were shocked by the senseless attacks and agonizingly long recovery process. Frank in particular was deeply upset watching

The Caldwell family celebrating Frank and Faye's 60th anniversary in 2000.
L-R Back: Heather, Shannon, Danita, Andrew, Jennifer, Mark Williams
(Jennifer's husband), Amanda, Tyler, Katie. Front: Dorothy and Myron, Neala
and Frank Jr., Frank and Faye, Tommy and Gloria, Dan and Pam, Carrie,
Kent Aldridge (Carrie's husband) holding great granddaughter, Madeline.

the daily news reports; tears filled his eyes. In the aftermath of 9/11, the U.S. and the world would never be the same.

If only 2001 could have ended on a happy note, but that was not to happen. On Christmas Day, Frank and Faye's lives were further derailed when Frank suffered a bad fall at home, shattering his left hip. He was hospitalized and underwent an operation requiring the insertion of metal plates and screws to repair the break. With grit and determination he endured twelve weeks of rehabilitation in a nursing center and finally returned to his longtime home on North Hoskins Road. He was even able to drive again, but over time Frank became more and more dependent on Faye and his children. A proud man, he fought valiantly to maintain his independence and dignity for the remainder of his life.

Slowed but not defeated, Frank lived independently with Faye for the next four years. While this new lifestyle was more difficult than what the two were accustomed to, they still shared a deep love for one another and continued to enjoy the company of their family. Frank planned and successfully surprised Faye with a party to celebrate her 80th birthday on April 4, 2004. A year later they celebrated their 65th and final wedding anniversary together with their children and grandchildren. Looking back over 65 years since eloping to York, South Carolina as teenagers, they felt blessed and proud to have a happy, healthy family that now included three great grandchildren and a fourth on the way.

Diagnosed with early stage prostate cancer many years earlier, Frank's initial treatments only required periodic injections to keep it at bay since it was a slowly growing cancer. However, over the last two years of his life, he frequently required medical attention, including radiation, as the cancer grew and spread to other areas of his body. In and out of the hospital several times during this period, he fought to regain his health, but the advancement of age, along with the cancer, and the impact of past surgeries proved to be too much. Weak and no longer able to eat, he was admitted to the hospital for a final time on February 7, 2006. The following day, the doctor confirmed his condition was terminal and told him there was nothing he could do, stating, "I wish I had better news to give you." Frank accepted the diagnosis with courage and grace, responding, "Well, I have good news. I am going to Heaven to be with my Savior."

During the four days of his hospital stay at least one family member was always with Frank, and on many occasions his hospital room was crowded with family and friends. There were busy and noisy times but also quiet ones, when the only sounds were Frank's sleeping slumber and the ticking of a wall clock. It was a time of sadness, laughter, memories, and reverence. Frank's hospital room became a place of worship as he told his family how much he loved them, that he was at peace with God, and that God loved them too. Just as he had done his entire life, at the end he was still giving to others, not concerned about his own condition.

Faye celebrating her 80th birthday with her boys in 2004.
L-R: Tommy, Dan, Faye, Frank Jr., Myron.

Frank and Faye celebrating their 65th wedding anniversary in 2005.

Frank's final wish was to die at home on the land where he had been born 85 years earlier. He returned home on February 10 under the care of Hospice to the house he and Faye built nearly 60 years before. Happy to be home, his last request was to have his family gather with him for one final family meal.

The next day, a Saturday, Frank and Faye's four sons, their wives, and the grandchildren arrived. Despite being confined to bed, Frank was content, speaking to every family member and sharing his love, faith, and wisdom. While Faye and her daughters-in-law were getting the food ready to serve, the Caldwell clan was as loud and noisy as ever, with family members scattered throughout the house laughing and talking. Taking it all in, Frank looked up and said, "Listen to them. Everyone is talking and no one is listening to anyone." With a big grin on his face he added, "That is what I like to hear!"

Over that weekend, Frank talked more than he had in months. Though his body was failing, his mind remained sharp. He explained, "This happened for a reason. God gave me this time to be with my family." He cherished that time talking with his loved ones, telling stories, and singing "Jesus Loves Me" with his grandchildren. At the end of his life he chose to die as he had lived—teaching and ministering to others about the things he considered most important, faith and family. Happy and content, he passed away the morning of February 17, 2006, a week after leaving the hospital.

Alone for the first time in her life, Faye moved from the home she built with Frank "out in the sticks" so many years before. As they promised Frank, her sons made sure she was taken care of and not left alone in her home. She sold the home on North Hoskins Road and purchased half a duplex in a small neighborhood in the nearby community of Oakdale conveniently located near her church and several friends. The family was concerned about the move, but Faye adjusted very well, getting to know many of her neighbors and enjoying the close proximity to church. For several years she lived independently in her duplex, actively participated in church, and frequently met with

Faye with her extended Caldwell family at her granddaughter Heather's wedding in 2010. L-R Back: Chad and Amy Caldwell, Jason and Amanda Fisher, Shirley Smith, Carrie Aldridge, Andrew, Jennifer, Frank, and Neala Caldwell. Middle: Tyler, Pam, Dan, Tommy, and Danita Caldwell. Front: Jennifer Williams, Madeline Aldridge, Cassidy Williams, Dorothy and Myron Caldwell, Heather and Stephen Moore, Shannon and Faye Caldwell, Jacob Aldridge, Gloria Caldwell.

a group of church friends for lunch and dinner. The family visited her often and continued to hold the traditional family gatherings at Christmas.

In the fall of 2010, Faye fell in her home, breaking her hip. After surgery and a period of rehabilitation, she lived in an assisted living facility until being hospitalized with a heart condition in early 2011. Her condition worsened during the hospital stay, and with all medical options exhausted, she was admitted to the Levine and Dickson Hospice House in Huntersville on February 2, 2011. Over the next several days one or more of her sons remained with her while family members and friends came to say goodbye. Although she never regained consciousness after moving to Hospice, she seemed to be holding on, waiting for her grandchildren to visit before she expired. She died on February 6, 2011.

When all is said and done, it's the simple things in life that matter most. Frank and Faye will never be hailed as important individuals in the great American story of the twentieth century. They didn't create any large businesses, hold political office, accumulate great wealth, or achieve celebrity and fame. Nevertheless, Frank and Faye were two among many millions of everyday Americans, the Greatest Generation, who loved and believed in God, country, and family, ultimately building the most powerful nation on earth. They lived the American dream, building a home of their own and raising a loving family. Jeff Pinkston, the Presbyterian minister who presided over their funerals, summed it up well, characterizing Frank and Faye as simple individuals who positively touched the lives of others. Jeff's words spoken at Frank's funeral were equally appropriate for Faye: "He was a man that the world will not much miss, but he was the kind of man the world so desperately needs."

Frank and Faye's wealth was invested in the love, faith, and hope they shared with family, friends, and each other. They left behind the most enduring legacies that stand the test of time—a loving family, good friends, and many happy memories. Two simple individuals who made a difference in the lives of many, Frank and Faye will always be remembered as humble and kind.

PERSONAL
RECOLLECTIONS

I grew up with three older brothers, Frank Jr., Tommy, and Dan, in a small three-bedroom house on North Hoskins Road in Mecklenburg County. Our only neighbors were family members, Caldwell relatives that included my grandmother, a great aunt and uncle, and three of Daddy's siblings and their families. It was a great place for kids, as we had the run of the Caldwell farm, playing in the woods, creeks, and pastures. Being the youngest of four sons, I missed out on some of the best years of life on the farm as much of it was sold, and the surrounding area developed, by the time I was a teenager. Even so, I fondly remember walking through the woods, fishing in the creek, and picking wild blackberries and muscadines. I often relive those memories in my mind, clearly retracing my steps on the farm in those simpler times.

Our Mama and Daddy were strict parents who established rules and maintained order within the family. Yet at the same time they were loving and nurturing, guiding us through our formative years, never imposing severe limits, and actually giving us a great deal of latitude to make our own way in life as we grew older. As strict as they were in my early years, I cannot recall them ever setting a curfew time when I went out for the night with friends during my high school and college years. For better or worse, our parents trusted us to do the

Daddy with me, Christmas 2005.

right things and be good people. We could not have asked for better role models.

Mama was the most loving person I have known. She was self-less to a fault, always understanding, and loved us unconditionally. Possessing the mind of an engineer and the skills of a craftsman, Daddy was incredibly talented. I always admired and respected him for his knowledge, steadfast character, and persistent work ethic. I frequently think about my parents and miss their love and wisdom.

Much of the information in this book is based on stories I heard over the years from my brothers and parents. I hope I have presented the facts accurately. With that said, it is impossible to capture all the stories and characteristics of the lives of individuals within a book. Following are some additional brief recollections and memories I have of my parents, Frank and Faye Caldwell.

Thursdays With Mama: For a long time my parents only had one car, which Daddy drove to work each day except Thursdays, when

Mama took him to work and kept the car to run errands and do the weekly shopping. When I was a little boy Thursdays were special, as I journeyed with Mama beyond our home to buy groceries at the A&P on Belhaven Boulevard and visit Grandma Lawing in Paw Creek. Mama usually treated me to a soft drink or a box of animal crackers while she shopped at the grocery store, and the visits with my grandmother always included cookies from her well stocked cookie jar. For a little boy like me, it did not get much better than that!

Sears: Sears, Roebuck and Company was one of the largest mail order and retail store chains in the U.S. for much of the twentieth century. Mama and Daddy were loyal shoppers, purchasing tools, car batteries, appliances, and clothes. As young kids it was a treat to ride with our parents to the Sears on 10th and Tryon streets on the edge of downtown Charlotte. My brothers and I enjoyed "riding" on the store escalator and marveled at the candy counter with its huge assortment of candy and nuts. I can still remember buying hot redskin peanuts, asking the "candy lady" behind the counter for "ten cents worth." No doubt the most memorable Sears experience was receiving the annual Christmas catalog, appropriately called "The Wish Book." Arriving in the mailbox several weeks before Christmas, the catalog showcased toys, clothes, and every gift idea known to man, easily making it the most read book during the Christmas season in the Caldwell family.

Mama Said It: Mama loved to talk to people whether they were friends, family, or strangers. She never had a problem starting a conversation, seemingly having an abundance of topics ready to spring on others. She had her own way with words and phrases that became well known among our family. A few are highlighted here:

"They have big jobs and make big money." A description attributed to anyone she believed was wealthy and financially well off. Mama often used this phrase to describe friends she knew as a child living in

Kendall Mill Village, who later moved to Coulwood, a nice neighborhood in Paw Creek.

"They are the nicest people." Defined as most of the people she associated with, but in particular those who lived in Kendall Mill Village and the members of Thrift Baptist Church.

"They wouldn't give you air in a jug." This was Mama's way of expressing her frustration with people who were stingy or greedy. By the way, most of these folks had big jobs and made big money, which grated on her even more. For those not familiar with air in a jug, air did not cost anything—at least not during her lifetime!

"Neat and clean." The minimum requirement to achieve the Faye Caldwell seal of approval. This statement was typically associated with people Mama met and observed, but also included houses, restaurants, medical offices, and hotel rooms. This term was most often used when she was surprised at how neat and clean the subject happened to be.

"That's real nice." This catchy phrase was used as an expression of approval or admiration for something others were discussing with or showing to her. Not surprisingly, she made this comment to her many grandchildren in almost every conversation they had with her!

Mama and me in 1964.

"Sit down and stay a while." Mama's greeting when someone stopped by on the spur of the moment for a short visit. She was always interested in extending those visits.

"*What's your hurry? You just got here.*" This was Mama's way of telling her visitors they were leaving too soon. It was a phrase she consistently used when her visitors were leaving, often several hours after they arrived.

"*Fixing supper.*" Simply how Mama communicated she was preparing supper. "Fixing" was a verb that typically described an action, and it was sometimes included as part of the two-word phrase "fixing to."

Mama and Daddy with Dorothy and me on our wedding day in 1983.

"*I just got my hair fixed.*" No, her hair was not broken. Fixed usually meant she had her hair shampooed, cut, or permed.

"*Those old people.*" This was a common phrase used in her later years to describe people her age or even years younger!

"*You know (her, him, them).*" Mama assumed I knew everyone she ever talked about. Many times I did, but often I did not, though that never stopped her from giving me the complete story about the specific individual or group of people I surely knew.

Sports Interests: Aside from church, family, and work, automobile racing was one of Daddy's greatest interests. He was a devoted follower of the NASCAR racing circuit, cheering for Richard Petty, his favorite driver. Only broadcast via radio in the early years of the sport, Daddy listened to the race commentators on his portable radio while relaxing on Sunday afternoons. He frequently attended NASCAR races at the Charlotte Motor Speedway in Concord and occasionally ven-

Daddy sitting with Mama on the front porch, radio in lap,
listening to the NASCAR radio broadcast in 1983.

tured to other nearby racetracks (North Wilkesboro, Hickory, Bristol, Rockingham, and Darlington) with one or more of his sons. He also enjoyed watching the "local boys" from the Charlotte area race on the dirt track at the Metrolina Fairgrounds on Statesville Avenue in Charlotte.

In addition to racing, Daddy faithfully followed his favorite National Football League team, the Dallas Cowboys. He admired and respected their coach, Tom Landry, a man of faith with high moral standards and a calm demeanor. On the other hand, Tommy, Dan, and I were avid fans of the Washington Redskins, the Cowboys' archrival. Washington and Dallas played twice a year and the games were always televised on Sunday afternoons, conveniently after Sunday lunch at our parents' house. Not surprisingly, there was a great deal of cheering and jeering among the four of us on those game days.

In Pursuit of Cloth, Buttons, and Patterns: Mama's love of sewing naturally evolved into a passion for shopping at her favorite fabric stores. Like it or not, my brothers and I became very familiar with those establishments. Her favorite was Mary Jo's Cloth Store, which began operations in the 1950s as a small store in Dallas, North Carolina. The store featured multiple rows of wooden tables covered with bolts of fabric and sewing supplies. Mama was a loyal customer for decades, and over that time Mary Jo's grew into a nationally known store. A promise of a soft drink or a candy bar usually appeased my brothers and me enough to overcome suffering through the experience while she admired the latest bolts of cloth, shiny buttons, and patterns. She would be sad to know that after more than 60 years, Mary Jo's Cloth Store ceased operations in 2019.

The Sunday Drive: Given his interest in cars, it is not surprising that Daddy loved to drive. On many Sunday afternoons, often on the spur of the moment, he would pile all of us into the car for a "Sunday Drive." The destinations were typically a short distance away in the vicinity of Charlotte. It could be a relative's house, a trip to drop off the payment for the "light bill" at the Duke Power drop box in downtown, or simply an impromptu drive through the countryside. Sometimes longer day trips were planned, usually to the nearby North Carolina mountains. Those trips typically included stopping at a roadside picnic table to enjoy lunch prepared by Mama.

Daddy with his car in the early 1940s.

Shopping with Mama: While sewing was Mama's favorite activity, shopping had to be a close second. Mama's oldest sister, Mae, was her most faithful shopping companion, joining her almost every Saturday morning for their shopping adventures. Their favorite destinations were Belk and Sears in the downtown area and Freedom Village Shopping Center on Freedom Drive. The shopping excursions often included lunch at their favorite restaurants: S&W Cafeteria, Shoney's on Freedom Drive, and The Old Original Barbeque House near Camp Greene Street. Mama loved browsing through the stores whether she bought anything or not. Always on the lookout for sales and good deals, she proudly displayed her purchases to family and friends, saying, "Look what I got on sale. Now that was a bargain!"

Shower and Shave: As mentioned earlier in this book, Daddy had a heart attack in 1993 when he was just shy of 73 years old. I was working in downtown Charlotte and received a phone call from Mama. She calmly asked me to drive to the house and take Daddy to the hospital because he might be having a heart attack. Concerned about getting him medical care as soon as possible, I suggested calling an ambulance, only to have my parents quickly dismiss that as not being necessary. I made the short trip in record time and rushed into the house anxious to get Daddy to the hospital. To my surprise he was not standing by the door ready to leave; instead, he was calmly shaving his face at the bathroom sink, explaining he needed to shower and shave before going to the hospital. He further added, "After all, this may not even be a heart attack!" His shave completed, he put on a shirt and the three of us sped to the emergency room at the hospital. The ER doctor quickly confirmed Daddy was having a heart attack, but until the end of his life he referred to this event as his "so-called heart attack."

Family Reunions: For many years the Lawing family held annual reunions on Mother's Day at Revolution Park in Charlotte on Remount Road. A large family, we practically took over the entire park with aunts, uncles, cousins, and close family friends gathering to catch up on the latest family news and enjoy food, games, and laughter.

Lawing Family Reunion at Thrift Baptist Church in 1968. Carrie Lawing and her children. L-R Back: Gene Lawing, Faye Lawing Caldwell, Loyah (Bud) Lawing, Rose Lawing Van Pelt, Carl Lawing. Front: Flo Lawing Thrower, Carrie Blankenship Lawing, Mae Lawing, Clifford (Peck) Lawing.

Attendance was always high and grew rapidly in the 1960s as many of my older Lawing cousins were married and starting their own families. The last few annual reunions were held at Thrift Baptist Church, across from Kendall Mill Village, where Mama lived as a young girl. In 1971 my grandmother, Carrie Lawing, attended her last Lawing family reunion before passing away the following year. She had twenty-three grandchildren and more than twenty great grandchildren at the time.

The Final Night at the Hospital: On February 7, 2006, ten days before he passed away, Daddy was admitted to Carolinas Medical Center. Knowing his time was short and not wanting him to be alone, my brothers and I took turns staying overnight at the hospital. On his final night there I arrived to stay and was joined later in the evening by Tommy. We filled the hours that night talking and laughing about old family stories and memories. I still remember as the night wore on and the conversations ended, the sound of Daddy sleeping and the clock ticking on the wall. Around midnight, we were all surprised when Dan, who had been on a business trip, came strolling into the room. Daddy was overjoyed to see Dan; he was the only one of his four sons he had not yet seen since being admitted. Reinvigorated, no one got much sleep that night as Daddy continued to talk well into the morning about various memories of his life, and we all sang "Jesus Loves Me." For the first time in almost 40 years, Tommy, Dan, and I spent the night together, reminding me of when the three of us slept in the same bedroom when we were kids. The next day we received the good news that Daddy could spend his remaining days as he wished, at home with his family.

The Frightening Driver: Living in Oakdale over the last five years of her life, Mama spent a considerable amount of time with two other widows, Evelyn Miller and Janie Helms, who lived in her neighborhood. All three were older than 80, owned their own cars, and were still driving. They enjoyed going to lunch and sometimes ventured out at night for dinner or to attend nearby church events. Mama often talked about how Evelyn, the oldest of the three, was not a very good driver and at times frightened her. On one occasion she told Tommy and me that Evelyn failed to stop at an intersection earlier that week, driving directly through a red light. Over time she continued to make comments about her neighbor's poor driving skills, so we asked, "Why do you keep riding with her if she scares you so much?" Without flinching or protesting she quickly replied, "Well, Evelyn is the only one of us who will drive at night!"

IN THEIR OWN WORDS

Mama and Daddy's favorite activity was visiting with their grandchildren. As I neared completion of this book, I asked their ten grandchildren to share memories and recollections of their grandparents. Their contributions provide a wonderful perspective through the eyes of their youth as well as later in life as adults. Initially planning to embed the comments within the prior chapters, I instead chose to include them here, in their own words.

Danita Caldwell

The three words that come to mind when I think about MawMaw and PawPaw are family, food, and love. They both loved to have the entire family as well as small family groups visit, and these visits almost always included food. Some of my favorite memories are from my childhood visits to their house for Sunday lunches and special holidays. The moment you walked into MawMaw's kitchen you were hit with delicious smells of food cooking and the sound of children playing and adults talking. By the time I was in high school, the family had expanded to more than twenty people. Tables were set up on the back porch and living room and you sat wherever you could find a spot, but you could hear a pin drop when PawPaw said the blessing. As soon as he was finished, the noise rose again until the entire house hummed with conversations. After the meal, we played inside and outside while the adults talked.

When it was time to leave, MawMaw always said, *"You don't have to leave yet, do you?"* even though we had been there for hours. Through their example, MawMaw and PawPaw created a legacy of love for family that continues to this day.

The Caldwell grandchildren at Frank and Faye's 50th anniversary in 1990. LR: Chad, Amanda holding Katie, Danita holding Tyler, Carrie holding Heather, Jennifer holding Shannon, Andrew.

Jennifer Caldwell Williams

PawPaw and MawMaw were two of my all-time favorite people. Living close by, we were blessed to spend a lot of time with them. I have so many fond memories. MawMaw and Dot Kiestler were my early Sunday school teachers. During "preaching," I remember looking up at PawPaw, who seemed like a giant to me, while he belted out the hymns. I would then lay my head on MawMaw's lap and she would play with my hair.

There were many Sunday lunches, and MawMaw always made a point to prepare what we liked. Nobody made better county style steak. I was always fascinated watching her cut up fruit or tomatoes, super fast, never using a cutting board. I remember PawPaw at the bar cutting up the meat. After lunch all of the kids would go outside, sit on the porch, and play the rock game, while everyone was talking at the same time.

When Andrew was born, kids were not allowed to visit in the hospital, but I remember waiting in the lobby of Charlotte Memorial with MawMaw for Daddy and Mama to bring him down for the trip home. I was wearing the blue coat she made me and was climbing on the furniture. She told me, "Quit wallowing, you're going to get filthy on this ole furniture. Watch that elevator." I listened and was so happy when that elevator opened and they were in it.

Another time, MawMaw and I took Andrew and Mama to Presbyterian Hospital when he was getting ready for his eye surgery. Allegedly, I threw a fit when it was time for MawMaw and me to go. I don't remember that, but I do remember MawMaw taking me out in front of the hospital. We filled her coat pockets and pocketbook with acorns. Afterward she bought me paper dolls, and all was right with the world.

Danita and I always had a summer sleepover with PawPaw and MawMaw. This involved a shopping trip with MawMaw, and we each got a dollar or two to buy "whatever we wanted." That was quite a laborious decision! We would fight over who got to sit by the door in the car, because of course we were all crowded in the front seat.

MawMaw was always up for shopping and loved to look for and talk about "bargains." When I was 16, Carrie 12, and Amanda 10, we were on one of those shopping trips at Eastland Mall and eating lunch at Chick-fil-A. I spontaneously asked if we could all get our ears pierced a second time. To this day I can't believe I asked her, and I really can't believe she agreed and consented for all three of us! Luckily, nobody could really get mad at MawMaw.

MawMaw was a talker. PawPaw would sit and listen, then he would start shaking his head and say, "Now Faye, you know that wasn't how it was, your Mama!" She would say, "Well, you tell it, Frank!" He would then proceed to retell the story. This always cracked me up. While

*Jennifer Caldwell Williams with MawMaw at
Caldwell Christmas in 2010.*

MawMaw was telling the story, she would be naming people and saying,
"You know 'em," and you might as well just agree, even though you often
didn't.

We went to a lot of events with them—funerals, weddings, and show-
ers. MawMaw would often call to see if Mama and I were "going to
wear britches." If Daddy answered he would always say, "Mama, I hope
they're going to wear britches."

I always looked forward to getting my winter jumper and my Easter
dress that MawMaw made. I remember two dresses she made when I
was older. She called and was so tickled (that's one of her words) about
how they looked. "They are so big! You're not going to be able to wear
these!" They looked better on. I loved those dresses. Although I don't
wear them anymore, I still have them in my closet, along with the blue
coat I mentioned earlier. I love, love, loved my MawMaw!

I always admired PawPaw. It goes back to those days looking up at
him in church. I was sure he could fix or build anything. PawPaw was
quiet and MawMaw talked enough for both of them, but don't be fooled:

as I said before, he was always listening. He was funny too, but you had to listen close or you would miss it.

PawPaw was tough. My husband, Mark, said he was a man's man, old school (those are compliments). He never really accepted he had a heart attack back in the '90s. I remember him talking to me about "that so-called heart attack" near the end of his days. That always made me laugh. PawPaw showed that hip fracture who was boss too. I hated him having to go to rehab, but I really enjoyed bringing him food and visiting him, one on one, on my way to work. He was always so grateful.

PawPaw was humble, kind, and super proud of his family. I remember when Cassidy was born, and he was not well. When I was taking pictures of her with him, he would always say, "Make it a good one." When he was dying, he said, "Bring that baby over here and let me see her." She would have loved him! I always think of him when I hear Alan Jackson's song, "Small Town Southern Man."

Frank and Faye enjoyed having all of their grandchildren over for family meals and special occasions like this gathering in 2001. L-R Back: Chad, Danita, Tyler, Jennifer, Amanda, Carrie. Front: Heather, Shannon, Andrew, Katie, Madeline (great grandchild).

Carrie Caldwell Aldridge

Writing my thoughts, memories, and what I learned from MawMaw and PawPaw is not easy for me. I can honestly say not a day goes by that I do not think about them. I can still hear their voices and the precise way they pronounced my name. That is something I wish to never forget. The way they felt when giving you a hug . . . I can still feel that too. The memories flood back constantly in my mind and in my heart. Their home was our opportunity to learn and grow, and just be a family. The many Sunday (and holiday) dinners and getting to play with our cousins was something I looked forward to. Looking back now I see what a blessing that was, and I hope to continue this with my children and grandchildren.

I can drift off with a smell, taste, or even a similar voice and it will startle me. Just like I think frankincense and myrrh smell like their bathroom. Silly, I know, but I have a small bottle of it, and it just takes me back into their home. In my mind I will walk through their home, room to room, where us kids played games, put together puzzles, and played dress up. I can walk around the outside of their home taking in every detail. Our imaginations soared playing in their yard. The clothesline quickly became a volleyball net, the rocks in the driveway became the rock game, and how quickly we could put together ball teams to compete with the adults. I spent many nights with them. Poor Grandma, she would have to sleep with me and Amanda. I remember her always laughing later in life about, "How in the world did the three of us ever fit in that bed?"

I wrote something a few years after MawMaw passed away. I think that it sums up what I learned from her. I can honestly sit here and say she was one of my best friends. On some days the pain of not having her here is still overwhelming for me:

When you take the time to sit back and reflect on the type of mother you are, you will realize that you have been shaped by all of the mother figures you have had throughout your life. You will often discover a little bit of each of them in yourself, having combined all their endearing qual-

ities you held so closely. My precious MawMaw, whom I miss so dearly, taught me the importance of eating together as a family. That was a place where everyone could talk about their day and say grace before touching their food. I learned from her that you may have little scraps of cloth, but when put together, they can turn into a beautiful piece of art. She taught me how doing for others could absolutely make someone's day . . . and mine too. I watched intently how she cooked, cleaned, and ran a household, providing an environment for her children and grand-children to be loved and cared for. At the end of the day there was always time for the most precious things in her life, the children. I learned from her how to be cautious and that things are not always what they seem. She showed me that it was okay to cry, and that crying right along with your children/grandchildren when they are hurt, scared, or just had a bad day was okay. The most valuable lesson I learned from her was the power of prayer, that prayers may not always be answered in the man-ner which you so desired, but nevertheless were always answered.

Christmas 2005 - Frank and Faye with their grandchildren and great grandchildren. L-R Back: Danita, Katie, Carrie, Amanda, Andrew, Tyler. Middle: Madeline, Jennifer, Shannon. Front: Heather, Frank holding Cassidy, Faye holding Jacob.

Andrew Caldwell

PawPaw always had an interest in politics as long as I can remember and consistently watched "This Week With David Brinkley" each Sunday after church. If he disagreed with the thoughts of a commentator, we knew it. For him to yell at the television was not uncommon. I always enjoyed that.

As I got older, I enjoyed showing up for family gatherings, walking through the back door, and hearing PawPaw holler my name. That would be followed by something like, "Get in here, boy!" I would immediately report to the living room, sit down on the chair next to his armchair, and talk a while.

Going to the race with PawPaw, Frank Jr., and Daddy [Tommy] was always fun. PawPaw would tuck his handkerchief under the back of his hat to avoid getting sunburnt on his bald head. He kind of looked like an Arab.

I liked the slow and methodical pace at which PawPaw consumed a meal. He appeared to truly savor every bite. It often made for some long restaurant experiences.

PawPaw often ensured proper television reception through banging on the side of the TV. An important life skill when cable is not available.

We frequently visited with the extended Caldwell family at MawMaw and PawPaws' house on Sundays. At Sunday lunch my Mama, Gloria, would load up my plate with a bunch of food I did not like. MawMaw knew this and, at some point, would always make her way to the back porch where I was seated, scrape the "bad food" off my plate into the trash can and say, "Don't tell your Mama!" I was very young at the time, but am still grateful to this day.

I always thought it was funny that MawMaw referred to her friend, Sarah Moore, by her full name . . . Sarah Moore.

Chad Caldwell

Probably the most important things that I learned from my grandparents were Faith, Family, and Hard Work. I don't remember ever hearing these spoken, but they were displayed all the time. When I told them that I had asked Amy to marry me, PawPaw shook my hand and said, "It's a good life." Four simple words, but so much weight and responsibility on them. And he was right. Something else I learned from him was that it is okay for a man to show emotion—to shed tears at a time the rest of the world says "boys don't cry." He was the manliest of men and wasn't afraid to show emotion.

As for MawMaw, I always remember the cooking. I've seen so many things that claim to be "better than grandma's," but I've never found anything to be "as good as MawMaw's." I do have to say that my mother-in-law makes the closest thing to MawMaw's potato salad, and it is the only potato salad I'll eat. Continuing in that vein, there was a time at a family gathering that MawMaw hadn't made her mashed potatoes. Andrew and I commented on this. I mean, they were the best mashed potatoes I've ever had! The next time we got together, MawMaw pulled us aside and told us she had made each of us our very own dish of potatoes to take home. The only thing better than MawMaw's mashed potatoes? Having an entire casserole dish of them to take home all for myself. And no, I didn't share! Hot fruit salad? I have the recipe . . . it's fine, but just isn't what I remember. Mac and cheese? Same.

I never knew/remembered my other grandparents, but I never once felt left out by that. MawMaw and PawPaw gave enough love, lessons, and memories to make up for anything I may have missed.

Amanda Caldwell

My favorite times were when we had "get togethers" playing ball in the side yard, sitting on the front porch with MawMaw counting cars, and playing hide and seek. Going to Hornets' Nest Park in MawMaw's car, sitting on those hot vinyl seats on summer days. Riding in the car with PawPaw, who acted like Richard Petty when merging onto I-85 or I-77 with Carrie and me bouncing all over the back seat. Waiting on PawPaw to get home from work, watching him pull in the driveway, and running from the front door to the back door to give him a hug. Getting up su-

per early to have breakfast with PawPaw before work: sausage, eggs, grits, toast, black coffee, and don't forget the slice of cake he had every morning too! MawMaw, Carrie, and me sleeping in the same bed. I still don't know how we all slept comfortably. Carrie and I getting up on cold winter mornings and sitting in front of the kerosene furnace to get warm. Sneaking an oatmeal pie or fudge cake when I wasn't supposed to, and getting caught when MawMaw found the empty wrappers I stashed under the bed. Making Barbie clothes from MawMaw's scrap fabric. Sitting in PawPaw's chair, watching Duke basketball games, and everyone, even MawMaw, yelling at the TV. Shopping with MawMaw, and the notorious ear piercing at Eastland Mall with Jenny and Carrie.

Tyler Caldwell

One memory that has stuck in my mind for years is when I was roughly eight years old and we were making the family photos. The photos were a surprise Christmas gift for MawMaw and PawPaw. My mind slips as to exactly how I did it, but I know I blew the surprise and told them along with several other people sitting in their living room.

A sad one is the morning PawPaw died. Once Dad and I found he had passed and told MawMaw, she cried for a brief ten seconds and then started asking us about getting laundry together. In a time like that, she was concerned about us being taken care of rather than taking care of herself. Perhaps it was a distraction for her, but I'll always remember that morning.

1997 - PawPaw with Heather and Tyler, taking a break from grilling.

Heather Caldwell Moore

MawMaw was always getting her hair fixed at the beauty shop, talking about who gave who down the country for what, asking us grandkids to give her some sugar, and of course telling every guest in her home "y'all don't leave now!" each time they left, no matter how long they'd been visiting.

Now PawPaw, who built that house she was telling everyone not to leave, may have been ready for us all to get out. As much as he loved his family, and that was evident to the end as we all gathered around his bed those last days singing songs about Jesus, he was a man of few words and, I imagine, ready for some quiet after the chaos of a big Caldwell family gathering.

They're embedded in some of my earliest memories: MawMaw buying me a Barbie when "I wasn't even 4 yet" (my mom's rule, gleefully broken by her mother-in-law), PawPaw putting me in "jail" or telling me he had a bone in his leg as if it were an ailment while sitting in his brown leather armchair in the den, taking Shannon and me out for Happy Meals, and going on vacation with us, wearing pants on the beach. There are so many other memories as I grew up, and it pains me that there won't be more. Playing in the bed of PawPaw's pick-up truck. Confiding in MawMaw about the latest sorority gossip while at Carolina. Hearing her concerned about planning to wear pants to my wedding around "those fancy Concord people." And even though they weren't here to meet my children, I still hear MawMaw's voice looking at their brown eyes: "Those are Caldwell babies."

Shannon Caldwell

As kids, Heather and I spent a lot of time at MawMaw and PawPaw's house. We always played a lot of games with MawMaw, like the rock game, "at me over," and picking a color to count cars that drove by (I usually picked my favorite color, purple, and always lost). Whenever we spent the night MawMaw insisted on lying on the couch in the bedroom, because she felt the need to stay with us until we fell asleep. This was concerning to me as a small child, as I thought MawMaw was a different person when she took her glasses off, which she often did when she laid down. Those glasses were just part of her signature look!

When we ventured out with MawMaw I remember thinking her car was the loudest I had ever heard. I recall telling mom about this, and her explaining the blinkers sounded really loud since MawMaw never played the radio! I also thought her car, a Dodge Spirit, was cool because she had automatic seatbelts and rolling windows. MawMaw often took Heather and me shopping and to visit her friends. She would take us to the dollar store, let us choose a toy and candy. I remember going to visit her friend, Mrs. Sides, often. MawMaw and Mrs. Sides were beside themselves when they saw our beanie babies, lamenting that they could have made those beanie babies!

MawMaw loved going out to eat, so taking Heather and me to McDonald's or Wendy's was a treat. I remember she wanted to go to Wendy's when the restaurant started selling "biggie" fries. So off we went, she and I splitting a "biggie" fry while Heather had the much smaller kid's meal fries. I was always a willing participant in MawMaw's schemes, but Heather was usually a little more reluctant. After PawPaw died, MawMaw continued taking us out to eat, though not for fast food. She never allowed us to pay for the meal, telling us, "I have money now. I can do this."

PawPaw was a bit of a softie with Heather and me. He would play with us from his chair in the living room, putting us "in jail," trapping us between his long legs. We thought this was so funny and would try to wriggle out of his grasp. He would also tease us, saying he had "a bone

Shannon with PawPaw at the Caldwell Christmas celebration in 2005.

in his leg." For the longest time, and being incredibly gullible, I thought this was a legitimate medical condition PawPaw had! As I got older, and PawPaw could no longer put me "in jail," I'd often sit with him and visit in the den. He always wanted to know what was going on in my life, especially with my various sports teams. He asked about the sports I was playing that season, how my teams were doing, how I was doing, etc. Our conversations were usually summed up with a succinct response of "Well, that's good."

Katie Caldwell Saville

What I remember and loved most about MawMaw was her caring and gentle nature. As soon as we'd pull up the gravel drive, she would come to the back door to greet us and tell us to come hug her neck. She always smelled of her favorite perfume, and that scent is embedded in my memory forever. I will never forget at my baby shower for Noah, we were sitting on the sofa together and she grabbed my hand and whispered in my ear, "I'm so glad it's a boy. Everyone keeps having girls. We need more boys." I guess that was the boy mom in her speaking, and now as a mom of only boys myself, I understand. We got a good chuckle out of that on the way back home that evening.

This is going to sound silly, but one of my favorite memories of PawPaw was the way he always yelled and talked to the TV. As a child, it was somewhat confusing, but now looking back it makes me laugh, especially because my father does the same thing. I also remember his strength and the way he would embrace me when he would "put me in jail." I loved that game and I adored that softer side of him!

Addendum 1

CALDWELL FAMILY GENEALOGY

Daniel Caldwell (1754-1827) – First Generation

Born in Argyll, Scotland, Daniel emigrated to North Carolina aboard the ship *Ulysses* in 1774. He settled in Mecklenburg County and married the widow Mary Howie Greenlee (1748-1825), also a Scottish emigrant, in the 1780s. Daniel's brother, Robert, and sister, Barbara, followed him to America and also lived in Mecklenburg County. Daniel and Mary lived in the Sugar Creek Community and attended Sugar Creek Presbyterian Church. Both are buried in the church cemetery on North Tryon Street across from the church. Daniel and Mary had four children (in this genealogy, the names in bold are the line of ancestry leading to Frank Caldwell):

- Robert Caldwell (1787-1853) married Susan Stafford (1789-1863)

- Samuel Caldwell (1788-1854) married Esther Barnett (1794-1883)

- **James Caldwell (1790-1839)** married Araminta (Minty) Beatty Parks (1796-1845)

- Mary Caldwell (1793-unknown) married William McGinnis (1793-unknown)

Daniel married his second wife, Elizabeth Dickson, in 1826, one year after Mary passed away. Daniel and Elizabeth did not have any children.

James Caldwell (1790-1839) – Second Generation

James was the third and youngest son of Daniel and Mary Caldwell, born in Mecklenburg County. He married Minty Parks in 1816. They lived on a farm along the old Concord Road (today known as Concord Huntersville Road) near the Cabarrus County line and were members of Ramah Presbyterian Church. James and Minty are buried in the church cemetery near the old entrance gate which was originally attached to a stone wall that encircled the graveyard. They had eight children:

- Daniel N. Caldwell (1817-1846)

- **William Caldwell (1820-1901)** married Margaret Johnston (1818-1846) first, Angelina Rebecca Templeton (1828-1897) second

- Mary G. Caldwell (1823-1903) married Caleb Barringer (1819-1897)

- Marcus Ephraim Caldwell (1824-1906) married Nancy Amanda Sloan (1834-1883)

- Elizabeth C. Caldwell (1828-1907) married Isaac J. Alexander (1826-1865) first, J.F. Kirksey (1836-unknown) second

- James Alfred Caldwell (1830-1920) married Hannah P. Stevens (1834-1868) first, Mary C. Wolfe (1833-1900) second

- Cyrus W. Caldwell (1833-1862)

- John Smiley Pharr Caldwell (1837-1897) married Margaret Rhea (1841-1924)

William Caldwell (1820-1901) – Third Generation

William was the second son born to James and Minty Caldwell on their farm in north Mecklenburg County. He married Margaret Johnston in 1844; she died only two years later. William married his second wife, Angelina Templeton, in 1851. They lived on his parents' farm until the late 1860s when they purchased Rosedale, a 629-acre plantation, and moved to the Alexandriana community. William and Angelina were members of Ramah Presbyterian Church until 1877 and Hopewell Presbyterian Church afterward. They are buried in Elmwood Cemetery just outside of downtown Charlotte. William and Angelina had nine children:

- Cicero Caldwell (1853-1855)

- Elizabeth (Bettie) Caldwell (1855-1927) married George Eggleston Woodruff (1851-1920)

- Ida Caldwell (1857-1858)

- Anna Caldwell (1860-1924) married Willard P. Dixon (1855-1896)

- **William Blake (WB) Caldwell (1860-1923)** married Lenora Jane Frazier (1865-1943)

- John Smiley Caldwell (1862-1926) married Anna Augusta Brown (1867-1945)

- Sallie Caldwell (1865-1932) married Joseph C. Lanyoex (1866-1931)

- Thomas Edney Caldwell (1869-1915) married Mary T. Grimes (1868-1966)

- Roberta Lee Caldwell (1870-1945) married Lemuel D. Whitsett (1848-1929)

William Blake (WB) Caldwell (1860-1923) – Fourth Generation

WB, the oldest son of William and Angelina Caldwell and the twin brother of his sister, Anna, was born on his parents' farm in Mecklenburg County. He married Lenora Frazier in 1885. WB and Lenora originally lived on a farm in Croft adjacent to WB's parents. In the early 1900s they moved to a 100-acre farm on Belt Road between Rozzelles Ferry and Beatties Ford roads. Here WB managed and operated the Caldwell Sausage Farm from the basement of his farmhouse. WB and Lenora attended Williams Memorial Presbyterian Church and are buried in the church cemetery. They had twelve children including an infant who died shortly after birth in 1908:

- William Frazier Caldwell (1887-1967) married Mary Jane Auten (1889-1929) first, Sarah Frances (Fannie) Auten (1895-1983) second

- **Thomas Parks (Tom) Caldwell (1889-1956)** married Azalee Wilson (1891-1975)

- John Raymond Caldwell (1890-1982) married Dora E. Coleman (1896-1951)

- Margaret Narcissa Caldwell (1893-1986) married Robert Roland Sloan (1892-1942)

- Angalene Caldwell (1894-1954) married Clyde Newell Neely (1897-1964)

- Willard Caldwell (1896-1958) married John Wilton Cross (1898-1968)

- James Albert Caldwell (1898-1972) married Elma McDowell (1898-1964)

- Mary Henderson Caldwell (1900-1971) married Raymond S. Six (1894-1969)

- Rebecca Templeton Caldwell (1902-1993)

- Isabelle Woodley Caldwell (1905-1976)

- William Blake Caldwell Jr. (1906-1984) married Kathryn (Kay) Lynch (1907-unknown) first, Bernice M. Buggie (1904-1984) second

- Infant Caldwell (1908)

Thomas Parks (Tom) Caldwell (1889-1956) – Fifth Generation

Tom was born in Mecklenburg County on the family farm in Croft, the second child of WB and Lenora Caldwell. He married Azalee Wilson in 1913. They purchased a small tract of land from Tom's parents and lived in a house located on the property. Tom and his brother Albert owned and operated the family sausage business under the name Caldwell Brothers Pure Pork Sausage following their father's death in 1923. Tom and Azalee attended Williams Memorial Presbyterian Church and McGee Presbyterian Church. They are buried in the cemetery at Williams Memorial Presbyterian Church. Tom and Azalee had six children:

- Sarah Elizabeth (Chuba) Caldwell (1915-2003) married Ernest David Bartlett (1905-1972)

- Lula Caldwell (1917-2011) married James (Jim) Henry Demarest (1916-1995)

- Thomas Parks (TP) Caldwell Jr. (1918-1939)

- **Frank Wilson Caldwell (1920-2006)** married Bertie Faye Lawing (1924-2011)

- Yates Templeton Caldwell (1922-1988) married Mary Edith Campbell (1926-2015)

- Esther Caldwell (1927-2003) married Jack Harding Correll (1921-1997)

Frank Wilson Caldwell (1920-2006) – Sixth Generation

Frank was the fourth child born to Tom and Azalee Caldwell in Mecklenburg County on the Caldwell farm between the Hoskins community and Beatties Ford Road. He married Faye Lawing in 1940. Frank and Faye built their home on a small tract of land purchased from Frank's parents in 1947. Frank worked in the Caldwell family sausage business for 22 years. Frank and Faye were longtime members of McGee Presbyterian Church, later becoming Pleasant Grove Presbyterian Church after merging with two other congregations. They are buried at Forest Lawn West Cemetery on Freedom Drive in Charlotte. They had four children:

- **Frank Wilson Caldwell Jr. (1943-living)** married Neala Johnston (1947-living)

- **Thomas (Tommy) Mack Caldwell (1948-living)** married Gloria Whitlow (1947-living)

- **Dan Vernon Caldwell (1952-living)** married Shirley Smith (1951-living) first, Pam Martin (1961-living) second.

- **Myron Lawing Caldwell (1957-living)** married Dorothy Roulston (1959-living)

Frank Wilson Caldwell Jr. (1943-living) – Seventh Generation

Frank Jr. was the first son born to Frank and Faye Caldwell. He married Neala Johnston in 1968. Frank Jr. received a doctorate degree in education from Clemson University. He taught in public school systems and at the college level for more than 40 years, spending most of his career at York Technical College in Rock Hill, S.C. He retired after many years as head of the college's Mathematics Department. Frank Jr. and Neala have two children and three grandchildren:

- Danita Arlene Caldwell (1973-living)

- Chad Michael Caldwell (1979-living) married Amy Denise Hart (1980-living) in 2002
  - Son, Drake Michael Caldwell, born 2005
  - Daughter, Teagan Denise Caldwell, born 2009
  - Daughter, Joceline Maelee Caldwell, born 2013

Thomas (Tommy) Mack Caldwell (1948-living) – Seventh Generation

Tommy was the second son born to Frank and Faye Caldwell. He served in the U.S. Army from 1968-1970 and is a Vietnam War veteran. Tommy married Gloria Whitlow in 1971. He worked for Norfolk Southern Railroad, retiring after 36 years of service. Tommy and Gloria have two children and one grandchild:

- Jennifer Ann Caldwell (1974-living) married Mark Caton Williams (1961-living) in 2004
  - Daughter, Cassidy Cheyenne Williams, born 2005
- Andrew Thomas Caldwell (1977-living) married Jennifer Ryan Lynch (1981-living) in 2007.

Dan Vernon Caldwell (1952-living) – Seventh Generation

Dan was Frank and Faye Caldwell's third son. He enlisted in the Air National Guard in 1970 and served six years in the reserves. He worked for Atlanta Hardwood Company, serving as company president upon retiring after 31 years. Dan married Shirley Smith in 1971. They have two children, two grandchildren, and one great grandchild:

- Carrie Anna Caldwell (1977-living) married Loyd Kent Aldridge (1975-living) in 1999
  - Daughter, Madeline Grace Aldridge, born 1998, married Tanner Owen Pennington, born 1998, in 2019
    - Daughter, Hazel Elizabeth Pennington, born 2019
  - Son, Jacob Loyd Aldridge, born 2003
- Amanda Kay Caldwell (1979-living)

Dan married Pam Martin in 1984. They have two children and three grandchildren:

- Daniel Tyler Caldwell (1986-living) married Jessie Annette Puckett (1982-living) in 2017
  - Son, Daniel Tyler Caldwell Jr., born 2021
- Katie Nicole Caldwell (1989-living) married Tyler Saville (1983-living) in 2013
  - Son, Noah Lucas Saville, born 2010
  - Son, Liam Carson Saville, born 2012

Myron Lawing Caldwell (1957-living) – Seventh Generation

Myron was the fourth son born to Frank and Faye. He earned a B.S. in Accounting from the University of North Carolina at Charlotte and became a certified public accountant. Myron married Dorothy Roulston in 1983. He worked in Finance at Duke Energy for 35 years, serving as a company officer for almost 20 years. Myron and Dorothy have two children and two grandchildren:

- Heather Eileen Caldwell (1987-living) married Stephen Abbott Moore (1986-living) in 2010
  - Son, Sawyer Abbott Moore, born 2017
  - Daughter, Grace Eileen Moore, born 2020
- Shannon Ashley Caldwell (1989-living)

Addendum 2

LAWING FAMILY GENEALOGY

William Lawing (unknown-after 1812) – First Generation

William, thought to be the first Lawing to live in North Carolina, was most likely living in Anson County in the 1750s, several years before Mecklenburg County was partitioned from Anson. He married a widow, Jean Killian Richards (unknown-after 1808) in the late 1750s. Jean had two children from her first marriage, John and Lizzie Richards. William and Jean lived in northern Mecklenburg County until around 1808, when they moved with several of their children to Warren County, Tennessee. They had eight children (in this genealogy, the names in bold are the line of ancestry leading to Faye Lawing Caldwell):

- **Andrew Lawing Sr. (1761-1825)** married Obedience Bradshaw (1765-1846)

- Elizabeth Susan Lawing (1766-1842) married Simon Hager (1763-1835)

- William Lawing Jr. (1770-1860) married Susannah Robeson (1760-unknown)

- Jane M. Lawing (1775-1859) married Solomon Stansbury (1755-1842)

- Mary Sallie Lawing (1775-1844) married Thomas Thomson (1767-1846)

- Ann Lawing (1778-1846) married Benjamin Allen (1773-1846)

- David Lawing (1778-1848) married Anny Sides (1786-unknown)

- Samuel Lawing (1782-1845) married Isabella Tassey (1794-1881)

Andrew Lawing Sr. (1761-1825) - Second Generation

Andrew was the first child of William and Jean Lawing. He was born in Anson County, North Carolina, one year before that portion of Anson was partitioned to form Mecklenburg County. Andrew married Obedience Bradshaw in the 1780s. He and his wife lived on a large farm near the Hopewell community in Mecklenburg County and attended Hopewell Presbyterian Church. Andrew served as a justice of the peace presiding over the Court of Common Pleas and Quarter Sessions in Mecklenburg County during the early 1800s. He is buried in Hopewell's cemetery beside the church. Presumably, Obedience is also buried there in an unmarked grave. They had nine children:

- David Lawing (1786-1856) married Elizabeth Prim (1798-1825)

- Robert Lawing (1788-1864) married Mary Ann Sublett (1797-1843) first, Ellen Ward (1827-1914) second

- John Killian Lawing (1790-1818) married Nancy Johnston (1789-1866)

- **Andrew Lawing Jr. (1793-1860)** married Elizabeth Phillips (1797-1850)

- Jane Lawing (1795-1854) married Samuel Hutchison (1794-1839)

- William Lawing (1797-1861) married Jane Waddell (1804-1866)

- Middleton Lawing (1800-1860) married Margaret Waddell (1805-1870)

- Samuel Lawing (1802-1865) married Amelia Dow (1810-1833) first, Susan Means (1815-1852) second, Eleanor Alexander (1818-1855) third, Jane Gibson (1815-1885) fourth

- Frances Killian Lawing (1805-1881) married Charles Hutchison (1796-1859)

Andrew Lawing Jr. (1793-1860) – Third Generation

Andrew Jr. was born in Mecklenburg County, the fourth child of Andrew Sr. and Obedience Lawing. Andrew married Elizabeth Phillips in 1813. They lived on a farm that was one of ten lots of property apportioned to Andrew Sr.'s heirs following his death in 1825. Andrew Jr. and Elizabeth likely attended Hopewell and Paw Creek Presbyterian Churches. It is not clear where they were buried, as no marked gravesites have been substantiated. They had 11 children:

- Jane Lawing (1814-unknown) married Francis Capps (unknown)

- Joseph Lawing (1815-1889) married Mary Scott Moore (1822-1900)

- Obedience (Biddy) Lawing (1816-1880) married William Moore (1815-unknown)

- Thomas Lawing (1817-1880) married Margaret Lawing (1822-1890)

- Jethro Lawing (1819-1864) married Sarah M. Cox (1819-1848) first, Margaret J. Reed (1828-1914) second

- Martha Lawing (1821-1895) married Andrew Hipp (1818-1862)

- Frances Lawing (1828-1888) married John L. Cook (1821-1912)

- Samuel E. Lawing (1830-1901) married Elizabeth A. Auten (1829-1874) first, Sarah M. Hinkle (1843-1928) second

- David F. Lawing (1833-1914) married Adaline Fidler (1832-1864) first, Sarah D. Robinson (1835-1876) second, Mary Smith (1853-1931) third

- William A. Lawing (1837-1916) married Ann Beal (1837-1923)

- **John Middleton Lawing (1841-1907)** married Elizabeth Beal (1842-1924)

John Middleton Lawing (1841-1907) – Fourth Generation

John was born in Mecklenburg County, the youngest child of Andrew Jr. and Elizabeth Lawing. He married Elizabeth Beal in 1860 and enlisted in the Confederate Army in 1862. John and his wife lived and farmed in Lincoln County, North Carolina after he returned from the Civil War. They attended Mountain View Baptist Church in Lincoln County and are buried in the church cemetery. John and Elizabeth had nine children:

- **Charles Forney Lawing (1861-1930)** married Dovie Ballard (1862-1914) first, Florence Moore Potts (1867-1931) second

- John Smith Lawing (1866-1956) married Laura Jane Caldwell (1871-1959)

- Oliver McDowell Lawing (1867-1939) married Nannie F. Killian (1874-1923)

- Dolphus Coleman Lawing (1870-1951) married Laura Killian (1872-1966)

- Mollie Elizabeth Lawing (1872-1951) married Ephraim Perkins (1870-1940)

- Edward Esley Lawing (1873-1950) married Martha J. Scronce (1873-1949)

- Caroline (Callie) Lawing (1877-1953) married Miles Elmore Shook (1872-1949)

- George Washington Lawing (1878-1942) married Emma Luzetta Lawing (1885-1959)

- Rueben Bertel Lawing (1884-1948) married Zanie Reynolds (1885-1961)

Charles Forney Lawing (1861-1930) – Fifth Generation

Charles Forney was born in Lincoln County, North Carolina, the oldest child of John Middleton and Elizabeth Lawing. He married Dovie Ballard in 1881. Forney and his wife farmed in Catawba County for most of their married life. They were members of Lawing's Chapel Baptist Church in Catawba County and are buried in the church cemetery. Charles Forney and Dovie had seven children:

- Cora Lawing (1882-1959) married Henry C. Keever (1875-1960)

- Bertha Lawing (1884-1936) married Charles E. Parker (1879-1938)

- **Charlie Mack Lawing (1887-1940)** married Carrie Nancy Belle Blankenship (1885-1972)

- Coleman Edgar Lawing (1891-1952) married Anna E. Yoder (1905-1966)

- Ruth Lawing (1893-1957) married William C. Turner (1892-1954)

- Hattie Lawing (1897-1958) married Eddie Lee Crafton (1894-1926)

- Garvin Odell Lawing (1901-1963) married Bertha Carswell (1902-1950)

Charles Forney married his second wife, Florence Moore Potts, in 1915, one year after Dovie passed away. Charles Forney and Florence did not have children.

Charlie Mack Lawing (1887-1940) – Sixth Generation

Charlie Mack was born in Catawba County, the third child of Charles Forney and Dovie Lawing. He married Carrie Nancy Belle Blankenship in 1907. Charlie Mack worked at Thrift Mill, later renamed Kendall Mill, located in the Thrift community in Mecklenburg County. Charlie Mack and Carrie attended Thrift Baptist Church and are buried in Forest Lawn West Cemetery in Charlotte. They had 10 children:

- Arnold Lawing (1908-1956) married Nell Scruggs (1909-2000)

- Ella Mae Lawing (1910-1978)

- Clifford Forney (Peck) Lawing (1912-1993) married Bernice Jordan (1913-1972) first, Nancy Pearl Abel (1915-2000) second

- Florine Lawing (1914-1996) married Clyde Adrian Thrower (1912-1975)

- Infant Lawing (1916)

- Rosella Lawing (1919-1997) married James Admiral Van Pelt (1915-1995)

- Loyah (Bud) Lawing (1921-2008) married Olga Klemchuk (1923-2005)

- **Bertie Faye Lawing (1924-2011)** married Frank Wilson Caldwell (1920-2006)

- Byron Eugene Lawing (1926-1993) married Charlene McGarity (1928-1985)

- Carl Vernon Lawing (1929-living) married Shirley Kirby (1935-living)

Bertie Faye Lawing (1924-2011) – Seventh Generation

Faye was the youngest daughter of Charlie Mack and Carrie Lawing, born in Mecklenburg County at Kendall Mill Village. She married Frank Caldwell in 1940. Frank and Faye built their home on a small tract of land purchased from Frank's parents in 1947. They were long-time members of McGee Presbyterian Church, later renamed Pleasant Grove Presbyterian Church, after merging with two other congregations. Frank and Faye are buried at Forest Lawn West Cemetery on Freedom Drive in Charlotte. They had four children:

- **Frank Wilson Caldwell Jr. (1943-living)** married Neala Johnston (1947-living)

- **Thomas (Tommy) Mack Caldwell (1948-living)** married Gloria Whitlow (1947-living)

- **Dan Vernon Caldwell (1952-living)** married Shirley Smith (1951-living) first, Pam Martin (1961-living) second

- **Myron Lawing Caldwell (1957-living)** married Dorothy Roulston (1959-living)

Frank Wilson Caldwell Jr. (1943-living) – Eighth Generation

Frank Jr. is the oldest son of Frank and Faye Caldwell. He married Neala Johnston in 1968. Frank Jr. received a doctorate degree in education from Clemson University. He taught in public school systems and at the college level for more than 40 years, spending most of his career at York Technical College in Rock Hill, S.C. He retired after many years as head of the college's Mathematics Department. Frank Jr. and Neala have two children and three grandchildren:

- Danita Arlene Caldwell (1973-living)

- Chad Michael Caldwell (1979-living) married Amy Denise Hart (1980-living) in 2002
    - Son, Drake Michael Caldwell, born 2005
    - Daughter, Teagan Denise Caldwell, born 2009
    - Daughter, Joceline Maelee Caldwell, born 2013

Thomas (Tommy) Mack Caldwell (1948-living) – Eighth Generation

Tommy was the second son born to Frank and Faye Caldwell. He served in the U.S. Army from 1968-1970 and is a Vietnam War veteran. Tommy married Gloria Whitlow in 1971. He worked for Norfolk Southern Railroad, retiring after 36 years of service. Tommy and Gloria have two children and one grandchild:

- Jennifer Ann Caldwell (1974-living) married Mark Caton Williams (1961-living) in 2004

- Daughter, Cassidy Cheyenne Williams, born 2005

• Andrew Thomas Caldwell (1977-living) married Jennifer Ryan Lynch (1981-living) in 2007

Dan Vernon Caldwell (1952-living) – Eighth Generation

Dan was Frank and Faye Caldwell's third son. He enlisted in the Air National Guard in 1970 and served for six years in the reserves. He worked for Atlanta Hardwood Company, serving as company president upon retiring after 31 years. Dan married Shirley Smith in 1971. They have two children, two grandchildren, and one great grandchild:

• Carrie Anna Caldwell (1977-living) married Loyd Kent Aldridge (1975-living) in 1999

- Daughter, Madeline Grace Aldridge, born 1998, married Tanner Owen Pennington, born 1998, in 2019

• Daughter, Hazel Elizabeth Pennington, born 2019

- Son, Jacob Loyd Aldridge, born 2003

• Amanda Kay Caldwell (1979-living)

Dan married Pam Martin in 1984. They have two children and three grandchildren:

• Daniel Tyler Caldwell (1986-living) married Jessie Annette Puckett (1982-living) in 2017

- Son, Daniel Tyler Caldwell Jr., born 2021

• Katie Nicole Caldwell (1989-living) married Tyler Saville (1983-living) in 2013

- Son, Noah Lucas Saville, born 2010

- Son, Liam Carson Saville, born 2012

Myron Lawing Caldwell (1957-living) – Eighth Generation

Myron was the fourth son born to Frank and Faye. He earned a B.S. in Accounting from the University of North Carolina at Charlotte and became a certified public accountant. Myron married Dorothy

Roulston in 1983. He worked in Finance at Duke Energy for 35 years, serving as a company officer for almost 20 years. Myron and Dorothy have two children and two grandchildren:

- Heather Eileen Caldwell (1987-living) married Stephen Abbott Moore (1986-living) in 2010
    - Son, Sawyer Abbott Moore, born 2017
    - Daughter, Grace Eileen Moore, born 2020

- Shannon Ashley Caldwell (1989-living)

SELECTED RESOURCES

Books

Alexander, J. B. *History of Mecklenburg County, 1840-1902.* Charlotte Observer Printing House, 1902.

Blythe, Legette, and Charles R. Brockman. *Hornet's Nest: The Story of Charlotte and Mecklenburg County.* McNally of Charlotte, 1961.

Ferguson, Herman W. And Ralph B. *Mecklenburg County, North Carolina Tax Lists 1977, 1798, 1806, 1807, 1808, 1811, 1815, 1823, 1824.*

Jenkins, Nell Bradford. *They Would Call It Ramah Grove: A History Of Ramah Presbyterian Church.* 1999.

Killian, J. Yates. *The History of the Killian Family in North Carolina,* 1940.

McDowell, Grace Bradford. *Record of Caldwell Family Collected and Recorded by Grace Bradford McDowell.*

Morrill, Dr. Dan. L. *History Of Charlotte and Mecklenburg County.* University of North Carolina at Charlotte.

Philbeck, Miles S. *Mecklenburg County, North Carolina Index to Land Surveys 1763-1768,* 1988.

Stolley, Richard B., Editor. *Time: Our Century in Pictures.* Bullfinch Press, 1999.

Thompson, Holland. *From the Cotton Field to the Cotton Mill, A Study of the Industrial Transition in North Carolina.* The MacMillan Company, 1906.

Tompkins, D. A. *History of Mecklenburg County from 1740-1903.* Charlotte Observer Printing House, 1903.

Manuscripts and Archival Sources

Ancestry.com

Chalmers Gaston Davidson Plantation Files, DC058. Davidson College Manuscript Collections.

Charlotte Mecklenburg Historic Landmark Commission Survey and Search Reports

Kenneth Wilson Whitsett Papers. J. Murrey Atkins Library, Special Collections and University Archives, University of North Carolina at Charlotte.

Mecklenburg County Register of Deeds. Charlotte, North Carolina. *Office Deed Books.*

North Carolina Division of Archives and History, Raleigh, North Carolina:

Wills and Estate Papers (Mecklenburg County) 1663-1978.

North Carolina Land Grants, Microfilm.

U.S. Census Records

Periodicals and Other Resources

Annual Report of the Bureau of Labor Statistics, 1938-1940.

Charlotte Mecklenburg Schools. *Long Creek Elementary, About Our School.*

Hill Directory Co. Inc. *Hill's Charlotte (Mecklenburg County, N.C.) City Directory 1940, 1947, 1961.* Hill Directory Co. Inc., Publishers, 1940, 1947, 1961.

Newsome, A.R. "Records of Emigrants From England and Scotland to North Carolina, 1774-1775." *The North Carolina Historical Review, vol. 11, no. 1,* 1934.

The Charlotte News

The Charlotte Observer

ABOUT THE AUTHOR

Myron Caldwell, a Charlotte native, enjoyed a long career in Duke Energy Corporation's Finance organization, retiring in 2016. The following year he accepted the best position ever: grandfather to his grandson Sawyer. Myron happily took on additional responsibilities three years later with the birth of his second grandchild, Grace. In addition to grandparenting, he enjoys time with his family, photography, researching family history, and traveling. Myron and his wife, Dorothy, have two daughters, Heather and Shannon, and live in Davidson, North Carolina, just north of Charlotte, with their dog, Reagan.

CPSIA information can be obtained
at www.ICGtesting.com
Printed in the USA
JSHW052042221022
32002JS00001B/1

9 781954 437746